THE TREE CLIMBER'S COMPANION

A REFERENCE AND TRAINING MANUAL FOR PROFESSIONAL TREE CLIMBERS

SECOND EDITION
REVISED AND EXPANDED

WRITTEN BY: JEFF JEPSON

ILLUSTRATED BY: BRYAN KOTWICA

The Tree Climber's Companion
Second Edition
Revised and Expanded

by Jeff Jepson
Copyright © 2000 Jeff Jepson

Published by Beaver Tree Publishing
1265 64th St. NE
Longville, MN 56655-9746
Email: beavertree@arvig.net
Web: BeaverTreeMN.com

November 2019 printing

Disclaimer

Serious injury or death could result from the use of techniques and equipment described in this book. It is the reader's responsibility to seek qualified instruction on the techniques and safety of tree climbing and tree work. Every person involved in tree climbing and tree work should use good judgment and common sense while practicing new techniques. Unfamiliar techniques should be practiced in a controlled environment before they are incorporated into everyday work procedures. This book is sold with no liability to the author, editor, publisher, or critiques, expressed or implied, in the case of injury or death to the purchaser or reader.

Cover design by Jim Clark

Library of Congress Control Number: 00-131772
ISBN 0-615-11290-0

This book is dedicated
to the memory of my Dad.
Richard Harding Jepson
1921-1999

.

Acknowledgments

For me climbing trees is infinitely easier and more enjoyable than writing a book, even a book about climbing trees. I often feel, during the writing process, a little bit like a bear on a bicycle. Garrison Keillor explains this notion best: "He (a bear) can be trained to do it for short periods, but he would rather be in the woods doing what bears do there."

The awkwardness the bear feels—I understand. And I realize that without the efforts of my "trainers" and helpers, this book would not be what I envisioned it to be. Therefore, I wish to offer my heartfelt thanks to the following: Ryan Pels for his crew leadership, competence, and willingness to do what is needed to get the job done; Jim Clark, Levi Durfey, Scott Peters, Tom Dunlap, Bryan Kotwica, and Kim Stay for their valuable assistance; all the climbers who offered suggestions for improving the content of this book; a special thank you to my wife, Bonnie, for her constant encouragement and support; and a very special thank you to each of my children, Anna and Luke, for reminding me every day of the things in life which matter most.

You have each, in your own way, helped the bear keep his balance long enough to complete the ride. Now he can go back into the woods where he belongs.

Preface

The Tree Climber's Companion has become an important part of my life since I first published it in 1997. In many ways it is like a tree, branching into several directions to cover the information that climbers need in order to operate safely and skillfully far above the ground. Just as a tree begins as a seed which must first germinate, this book began as an idea, a conviction really, that my passion for climbing and rigging safely could be effectively conveyed to those in my industry who wish to be safer and more productive workers. With the encouragement of fellow professionals, my idea took root and grew into the first edition of this book. It surpassed my expectations in sales and, more importantly, in the positive response it generated from professional tree climbers. It served as a classroom reference for tree climbers and as a knot reference manual. Best of all, it functioned as a compact field reference for those with whom I share my passion, professional climbers who rely upon rigging knowledge and climbing skills to earn their living in trees.

My desire to publish a second edition of *The Tree Climber's Companion* emerged from reflections of a rather serious fall I suffered while performing a routine removal of a large, hazardous Jack Pine in 1994. To this day I can remember nearly every detail of that fall and the many violations of safe climbing practices I committed which preceded it. Forty feet above the ground, secured to the trunk of the tree with only a single lanyard, I was limbing the smaller branches of the big Jack. That's when it happened. As I reached to cut a branch, operating the saw with only one hand, my leather glove caught in the throttle trigger, keeping the saw accelerated after I had cut through the limb. To my horror I was unable to stop the saw's downward progress. I watched in disbelief as I accidentally cut my own lifeline, the safety lanyard securing me to the tree. In the ensuing eternity of seconds I cartwheeled through the tree to the frozen ground below. What followed was a long wait for an ambulance, a lengthy session of x-rays and the most amazing sense of peace and awe I have ever experienced as I thought of God's awesome power and His ability to rescue me from a helpless and seemingly hopeless situation.

In Exodus 33:19 God proclaimed to Moses: "I will have mercy on whom I will have mercy, and will have compassion on whom I will have compassion." As I was lying on the x-ray table I knew that I had just experienced both God's mercy and His compassion. The doctor confirmed this a short time later when he reported that the x-rays revealed nothing broken. He called it my "lucky day."

The incident was not a conversion event; I had been a Christian for years. But, just as a tree grows into its purpose, so do the events that shape us. I have published this book once believing it to be a call to others to climb safely and skillfully. I publish it again with a greater purpose of also encouraging my fellow climbers to transcend the immediate. As climbers of trees we live precariously, with a real need to practice safe climbing techniques. As people we also live precariously if we fail to prepare for the event which has eternal significance. We can prepare for that event today by attaching our personal safety lanyard to the One who creates the trees we love and who grants mercy and compassion to those who climb them.

Introduction

Most of the people who read this book will bring to the experience a love of both trees and climbing. They may or may not be accomplished in the skills it takes to climb well, but they will probably have a keen appreciation, honed over time, for the effort it takes to gain a new vantage point. I sense that most climbers have always been climbers in their hearts. They were the risk takers in childhood who never let fear, or common sense perhaps, displace the feeling of exhilaration they got when they finally reached the highest point in the tree.

This book is for them and for all who wish to climb and work safely in trees. This book is intended to help everyone minimize unnecessary effort and maximize productivity, not just over the course of the day, but over the course of a lifetime. It is not a book that provides shortcuts at the expense of safety. Instead it is a book that promotes safe operation as the true shortcut, the best method of completing a task efficiently with the lowest risk of injury.

Those who read the first edition of this book will recognize this effort as an expansion of the first. It now includes over 200 illustrations, expanded information on all the original topics, more sidebars and several detailed explanations of key "Tools of the Trade." I have also added additional knots, expanded the list of information sources, listed arborist equipment suppliers and added some handy skill performance sheets. These additions provide climbers with a more complete reference and training guide. I believe the additions still allow the book to be used efficiently and stored conveniently, close at hand.

As an author, I want people to benefit from this book, and I believe that most who read it will. However, this book was never intended to be a sole source of information for climbers. Others have written similar books, and true professionals will maintain a library of quality resources. I also strongly encourage climbers to attend climbing jamborees/competitions and workshops so you can rub shoulders with other experienced climbers. Each has a wealth of information to share. In addition I recommend that climbers join the professional organizations which promote our profession. The International Society of Arboriculture and the Tree Care Industry Association are two organizations that help educate climbers through newsletters, magazines, training videos and books. They do a good job of keeping us informed of the issues affecting the profession.

Finally, I would like to say that this book is also a tribute of sorts to the profession, itself. It is a recognition that working safely in trees requires a better understanding of trees and techniques than we ever could have imagined necessary when we were those risk-taking youngsters pushing ourselves to the highest vantage point in the tree. While we have not let fear displace the sense of exhiliration we feel during our climbs, we have let common sense temper our judgement. This book will let you put that common sense to great use. It will also let you find that sense of exhiliration time and time again, confident of your abilities and mindful of the respect it takes to operate successfully. It will show you that safety is an attitude about your job and the trees we love. Our profession deserves no less.

Gearing Up

For a safe and productive climb, it is essential that the climber use tools and wear clothing suitable for the climbing and work situation. The modern tree worker has a wide variety of climbing gear and clothing from which to choose. Each item has a specific and sometimes multi-purpose function. Determine for yourself which tools and clothing will best meet your climbing needs. Explore the potential of each one and become proficient in operating and maintaining it.

For starters, tree workers can significantly reduce the chance of personal injury simply by using common sense and wearing proper safety equipment such as head, eye, and hearing protection. This equipment is referred to as personal protective equipment or PPE. But it's not enough to simply wear it; this equipment must be inspected and cared for properly and regularly. The employer and employee are held equally responsible for the safe working condition of this equipment and the enforcement of its use.

There is other PPE that the tree worker needs to consider, such as hand protection, footwear, clothing for everyday field use, and clothing offering protection from chainsaws. The selection of these items is dependent on the job, the climate, and the requirements of the employer.

The climber on the opposite page is well equipped and safely dressed for climbing trees. These "tools of the trade" are examined in more detail and appear throughout the book, particularly within the discussion of the climbing technique where the tool is most likely to be employed. Use the illustration as a visual checklist and quick reference for locating and learning more about the climbing gear discussed in the pages that follow. Since the discussion of tools is limited in this book, it is recommended that the reader seek out other sources of information, listed on pages 94-95, to obtain a more detailed account on the use and maintenance of climbing gear. Don Blair's *Arborist Equipment*, for instance, is unsurpassed in its presentation of climbing equipment and should be considered required reading for all tree climbers and workers.

Only by experience, training, and experimentation will the novice tree worker ultimately determine which climbing gear to use. Simply paging through a current arborist equipment catalog (see pp. 96-97) and reading the product description will provide valuable information and insights on what the most popular "tools of the trade" are. Of course, catalogs also provide a convenient way of purchasing the tools as well. Also, talking with other arborists and finding out their equipment preferences could save the novice tree worker a lot of trial and error.

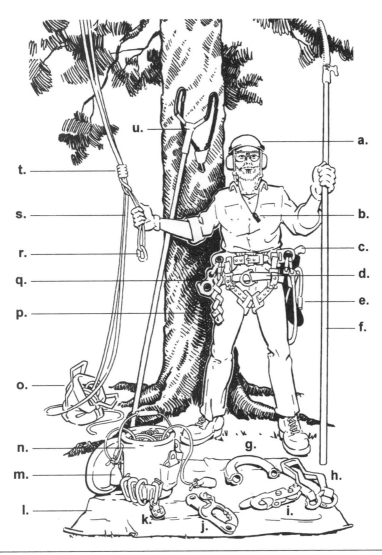

Key to Climbing Gear

a. Personal protective equipment, pp. 8,12
b. Whistle, p. 58, sidebar
c. Hand saw
d. Climbing saddle, p. 13
e. Personal lanyard & length adjuster, pp.13, & 38-39
f. Pole saw, pp. 33,56
g. Rope saver, pp. 30,52
h. False crotch, pp. 27-29
i. *Petzl Stop*, pp. 64-65
j. Handled ascender, p. 47
k. Micro pulley, p. 55
l. Rope tarp, p. 15
m. Throwline/bag, pp. 20,56
n. Rope/gear bucket, p. 14
o. Rope bag, p. 14
p. Webbing sling, pp. 62-63
q. Figure-8, pp. 64-66
r. Double-locking carabiner, p. 13
s. Climbing line, pp. 12,78
t. Prusik loop, pp. 90-91 (knots, pp. 67-93)
u. The Big Shot, p. 23

The P.R.E.P. Tree Climbing System

The P.R.E.P. tree climbing system is a step-by-step procedure that enables arborists to climb, work in, and descend trees safely and efficiently. This system follows a logical sequence of action providing the climber with numerous techniques to fit a variety of climbing situations. This climbing system was devised for and used successfully in training workshops by beginner and experienced tree climbers alike.

The old adage, "a chain is only as strong as its weakest link," is a relevant principle when climbing trees. Like the "weak link" in the chain, failure to perform or be proficient in any of the steps in this climbing system could result in disaster or, at the very least, an unproductive climb. The success of a climb and proposed work plan hinges on the skillful execution of each step of the P.R.E.P. climbing system as well as the appropriateness of the technique chosen for the situation. The pages that follow discuss in detail each step and technique of the climbing system outlined in the flow chart below.

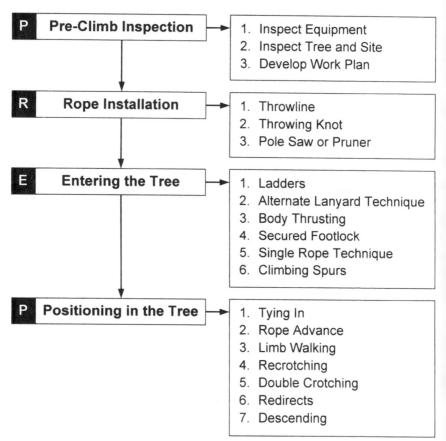

P Pre-Climb Inspection	→	1. Inspect Equipment 2. Inspect Tree and Site 3. Develop Work Plan
R Rope Installation	→	1. Throwline 2. Throwing Knot 3. Pole Saw or Pruner
E Entering the Tree	→	1. Ladders 2. Alternate Lanyard Technique 3. Body Thrusting 4. Secured Footlock 5. Single Rope Technique 6. Climbing Spurs
P Positioning in the Tree	→	1. Tying In 2. Rope Advance 3. Limb Walking 4. Recrotching 5. Double Crotching 6. Redirects 7. Descending

P—Pre-Climb Inspection

The first step in the P.R.E.P. tree climbing system is the pre-climb inspection. Most accidents that occur during tree climbing operations could be avoided by giving careful attention to the pre-climb inspection. This inspection must be made routinely, systematically, and thoroughly before a tree is climbed. The pre-climb inspection consists of these steps:

1. **Inspect Equipment**
2. **Inspect Tree and Site**
3. **Develop Work Plan**

In the pages that follow each step is covered in more detail and provided with inspection checklists to facilitate the process. Feel free to make copies of these checklists to be used in the field. They may also prove useful for field arborists involved with developing the work order/estimate. Devise a check off system that is suitable to your needs.

ANSI: The Bottom Line on Safety

Safety is one of the primary goals of the tree climber and ground worker. Consulting **ANSI Z133.1** is a wise first step toward meeting that goal. This is a publication of safety standards for tree care operations published by the American National Standards Institute or ANSI. ANSI Z133 is the recognized safety standards for tree care operations in the United States. These safety standards are developed and updated on a regular basis by a committee of tree care professionals (Accredited Standards Committee or ASC). With the continued rapid evolution of climbing techniques and equipment used in the tree care industry, there will also come additional revisions from the ASC committee regarding their use.

Although the publication refers to the standards as requirements, compliance is voluntary. Nevertheless, the ANSI Z133 publication is the industry consensus for safety. The prudent tree climber, ground worker, and employer should read, learn, and practice these guidelines.

The safety requirements discussed in this book are derived from the ANSI standards. The words **should** and **shall** are important and consistent words that appear in the ANSI standards. Shall denotes a mandatory requirement whereas should denotes an advisory recommendation. Reference to ANSI is included in this book on a limited basis. Therefore, the climber, ground worker, and employer is encouraged to obtain a copy of the ANSI Z133-2012 publication (the most current edition the time of this reprint) and read it thoroughly.

1. Inspect Equipment

The pre-climb inspection begins with a thorough inspection and maintenance of all climbing equipment each day before use. Not only is it a prudent practice but one required by ANSI Z133.1-2000. Defective and damaged equipment, or equipment showing signs of wear and deterioration, should be removed from service or, when acceptable, repaired before being put back into operation.

The equipment inspection needs to be an ongoing process that occurs not only before climbing but during and after the climb as well. Inspecting equipment should become second nature and performed often, especially when equipment becomes subjected to potentially damaging situations during the climb.

EQUIPMENT INSPECTION CHECKLIST

Personal Protective Equipment

☐ Check head protection ("hard hats" or safety helmets) for cracks, frayed straps, or any other sign of wear or damage to the shell or suspension.

☐ Make certain that ear and eye protection is functioning properly and in serviceable condition.

☐ Find out if the clothing, footwear, and gloves (also chainsaw protective clothing and back support belts) are appropriate or required for the work location and situation. Inspect for tears, holes, or wear that could interfere with safe work operations.

Rope: Climbing, Rigging, and Split-Tail Lines

☐ Ensure that arborist climbing lines have a minimum diameter of 1/2 inch/12.5 mm (see ANSI Z133.1-2000 section 3.5 for exception) and a minimum breaking strength of 5,400 pounds (24 kN) when new. (Split tail and Prusik cord may be less than 1/2 inch diameter.)

☐ Inspect lines for glossy or glazed areas (heat damage), inconsistent rope diameter (internal damage), discoloration (chemical contamination), and stiffness (exposure to pine pitch).

☐ Check for cuts, puffs (pulled strands), and areas of excessive fraying.

☐ Ensure that rope ends are sealed by melting, taping and/or whipping to prevent unraveling.

☐ Regularly rotate the climbing system from one rope end to the other. Cut off worn rope ends when necessary.

Inconsistent diameter

Puff

Excessive fraying

Evidence of rope damage

Climbing Saddle

☐ Inspect saddle for cuts in material, abraded webbing, and broken stitching.

☐ Check to see that rivets and grommets are not loose, bent, or missing.

☐ Inspect buckles, D-rings, and hooks for cracks or any sign of distortion.

☐ Check for elongated holes in waist strap.

Personal Lanyards, Fliplines, and Prusik Loops

☐ Make certain that Prusik loops and lanyards meet minimum strength standards required for climbing lines (5,400 pounds).

☐ Inspect rope lanyards and Prusiks for wear as you would climbing lines.

☐ Examine lanyard terminations used to secure the connecting device (carabiner, rope snap, or screw link): inspect back splices, rope, and wire eye splices for wear. Ensure that knots are tied, dressed, and set properly.

☐ Ensure that the length adjuster is functioning properly. Replace "quick lock" pins found on Gibbs and Microcenders with a bolt and lock nut. If a friction hitch is being used as a lanyard adjuster, check for signs of wear.

Carabiners, Rope Snaps, and Screw Links

☐ Make sure the connecting devices used for tying in to the climbing line have a minimum breaking strength of 5,000 pounds and require two separate and distinct motions to open ("double-locking").

☐ Ensure that surfaces are free of cracks, sharp edges, corrosion, burrs, or excessive wear. Hand sand any burrs with 220-400 grade sandpaper.

☐ Make sure gates open and close quickly and easily. Be sure the locking mechanism closes freely and completely. If sticking occurs, use an air hose to blow out grit, wash in warm soapy water, rinse, and lubricate with dry graphite around the hinge area, spring hole, and locking mechanism.

☐ Rivets must not be bent, loose, or missing. Discard if found defective!

Miscellaneous Climbing Equipment

☐ Inspect ascending and descending devices for wear and proper operation.

☐ Inspect redirects and false crotch devices for wear.

☐ Check blocks (pulleys) for proper operation. Sheaves must turn freely but without excessive play. Make sure bolts are tightened adequately.

☐ Avoid placing any climbing equipment directly on the ground where sand, dirt, mud, and water are present. Use rope and gear buckets, bags, and tarps instead to organize and protect gear from the elements (p. 14).

Tools of the Trade: Buckets, Bags, and Tarps

How climbing equipment is stored and organized greatly affects its working condition, life span and, in the case of climbing lines and throwlines, ease of deployment. Buckets, bags, and tarps keep climbing lines and gear away from direct contact from the ground while they are being used and are also a means of storage. Perhaps the most virtuous feature of any of the three methods is the ability for a climbing line or throwline to pay out smoothly without tangles when it is deployed. They also allow the climber to use only the amount of rope or throwline necessary to perform the job, without subjecting the rest to moisture, dirt, and piles of brush.

Regardless of storage method, climbing lines in particular need special attention. They should be stored in a clean and dry environment, away from direct sunlight, off concrete or dirt floors, away from extreme heat, and away from chemicals and fuel. It is recommended that wet ropes be coiled (p. 69) and hung up to be dried before storing in a bucket, bag, or tarp.

Gear Buckets

Gear buckets consist of a pocketed sleeve that fits over a 5-gallon paint or "mud" bucket. The pockets, located inside and out, allow users to organize gear in a manner that meets their needs. Many climbers use the main compartment to store their throwline or climbing line (up to a 120 ft of 1/2 in. line) and utilize the pockets to store such items as extra throwbags, carabiners, pulleys, as-

Buckets are handy gear organizers.

cenders, chain saw wrench, felling wedges, etc. The bucket can be fitted with a lid that protects the interior from the elements and furnishes a seat for rest.

Rope Bags

Most rope bags do not allow for good gear organization and are therefore used mainly to store rope and throwline. Rope bags are, however, very durable, able to withstand the abuse of being thrown from the tree or having limbs dropped on them. Like the bucket, lines are stowed by stuffing, allowing for tangle free deployment the next time the rope is used. The most user friendly rope bags are stiff enough to stand up on their own while the climber stuffs in the line. There is a wide range of sizes available to accommodate a range of rope lengths. The smallest bags can be stuffed with nylon throwline and attached to the climber's saddle. Rope length and type can be identified by using different colored rope bags. Most designs have a drawstring top to secure and protect the contents and some even integrate outside pockets for limited tool storage.

Stuffing rope in a bag takes no longer than coiling and when put to use pays out from the bag without tangles.

Small storage bags, termed by one manufacturer (New Tribe, p. 97) as a "Linemug", are used to store nylon throwline. They are compact enough to attach to the climber's saddle where it is available to perform chores while climbing aloft.

Rope Tarps

Rock climbers have popularized the use of rope tarps and they have caught on with tree climbers as well. With a tarp, climbers "flake" or pile the rope (or throwline), instead of stuffing, onto a much larger target than what buckets and bags furnish. This feature also allows the climber to flake the rope onto the tarp as it is being cleared from the tree. This saves time and protects the rope from ground contact. Most rope tarps accommodate gear storage as well. After stowing the line, the tarp is folded and secured with carrying straps or stored in its own attached stuff bag. Some designs have shoulder straps allowing it to be transported like a backpack, freeing the climbers hands to carry other equipment. Tarp sizes vary, but one measuring 3x5 feet will easily handle 120 feet of 1/2 inch rope.

What About Suitcases?

Tom Dunlap is an arborist and innovator who is always adapting household junk and garage sale finds into useful climbing gear. His creations often invoke a quizzical response from other climbers. However, his application of old suitcases used as a container for storing anything from ropes and climbing gear to lunch and a hammock is, in my opinion, a discovery truly worth sharing.

I picked up my suitcase at a garage sale for $3.00. It now conveniently houses a 150 ft climbing line, a false crotch, half a dozen "biners," a pair of handled ascenders, throwline, and a lightweight climbing harness. I especially like how it opens up revealing the entire contents at once. I plop it down under the tree I'm climbing, take out what I need, and zip up the rest. It may be ugly, but it's a work horse.

2. Inspect Tree and Site

Visually inspect each tree completely from the ground for potential hazards before you climb or begin work. Examine all "sides" of the tree from the roots to the branches. A careful examination of the climbing and work site is also necessary. Most property damage results from neglecting this part of the pre-climb inspection.

Tree foliage will often obstruct the view of tree hazards hidden within the canopy. The use of binoculars will assist in locating them. As you climb and perform work aloft continue to perform a visual inspection of the tree, watching for problems which were not visible from the ground. In addition, be attentive to sounds that could indicate a potential hazard such as the buzzing of hornets and bees or any other animal noises.

Use the checklist on the following page to help locate the tree and site hazards illustrated above. Identify the crotch most suitable for rope installation mindful of these known hazards.

TREE AND SITE INSPECTION CHECKLIST

Root Zone

☐ Mushrooms present at the base of tree (sign of root rot)

☐ Cracks near root flare

☐ Lack of root flare

☐ Soil mounding (tree failing)

Trunk

☐ Mushrooms and conks

☐ Cracks and cavities (use a rubber mallet for "sounding" the trunk)

☐ Vines—can be poisonous (poison ivy/oak) and often obscure other hazards

☐ Loose bark

☐ Swellings or depressions

Tree Crown

☐ Hangers (lodged branches)

☐ Dead and weak branches

☐ Weak branch attachments

☐ Cracks/splits along stem, branch, or where branches are attached

☐ Stinging insects (look and listen)

☐ Animals (look and listen)—rap on trunk with mallet to arouse activity

☐ Electrical conductors (often concealed by foliage and therefore are not readily visible)

Storm Related Situations

☐ Tree parts under points of pressure and tension

☐ Lodged branches—be particularly alert for hangers found near or blocking the climbing route.

☐ Ice, snow, or wet limbs—create slippery climbing conditions and hide tree defects

Climbing and Work Site

Look for potential targets, obstructions, and hazards such as:

☐ Structures: buildings, decks, etc.

☐ Vehicles (parked or moving)

☐ Sidewalks and driveways

☐ Septic system and drain fields

☐ Presence of lawn ornaments, lawn furniture, clothes lines, play areas, bird feeders, and landscape lighting

☐ Young trees and shrubs, flower beds, and other landscape items

☐ Satellite dishes and antennas

☐ Electrical hazards

☐ Wet and muddy areas

☐ Poisonous plants

☐ Extreme slopes

☐ People in the area (homeowner, bystanders)

Tree and site hazards from page 16: 1) Wet, marshy area 2) Mushrooms at tree base 3) Cavity at tree base 4) vines—poison ivy? 5) Mushrooms/conks on trunk 6) Split in branch 7) Large dead wood 8) Split branch union 9) hornets nest

3. Develop Work Plan

The final step of the pre-climb inspection is the development of a suitable work plan. This plan involves: 1) having a thorough understanding of the work order/job description, 2) ensuring the proper equipment is available and functioning properly, 3) ensuring that the climbing/work site is safe and finally, 4) determining the entry route and entry method. Use the checklist below to assist in developing the work plan.

CHECKLIST FOR DEVELOPING A WORK PLAN

The Work Order/Job Description

☐ Make sure that the instructions on the work order have been clearly communicated and understood by all the workers involved with the job.

☐ Determine the location of the work to be performed.

☐ Determine the most efficient order to perform the work.

The Gear

☐ Make certain that all the necessary equipment to climb and perform the work aloft are readily available and in safe working condition.

☐ Have aerial rescue and first-aid gear on site.

☐ Warm up chain saws on the ground before they are sent up into the tree.

The Climbing and Work Site

☐ Locate a drop or landing zone for dropping and rigging down wood.

☐ Ensure that the work site is safe by either moving targets or protecting them with plywood, tarps, tires, or other aids.

☐ Warn customer and any bystanders of work to be performed.

☐ Use safety cones, signs, flagging, and/or a grounds person to keep people away from the work area.

The Entry Route and Method

☐ Select an entry route that is free of any hazards discovered during the tree and site inspection (electrical hazards, hangers, stinging insects etc.).

☐ Select an entry route that provides the best path to the tie-in point.

☐ Select a route on the side of the tree away from existing electrical conductors and other potential hazards.

☐ Locate a tie-in point for a rescue line. Consider installing the rescue line before climbing the tree.

☐ Determine method of entry. The entry route chosen strongly influences this decision. For example, is the entry route close to the trunk (body thrust or ladder) or distant (single rope technique, secured foot lock)?

R—Rope Installation

Rope installation is the process of setting a climbing line from the ground over a suitable crotch in the tree. This line will provide access for climbers using the body thrust, secured footlock, or single rope technique. The climber has several rope installation options from which to choose including the following:

1. **Throwline**
2. **Throwing Knot**
3. **Pole Saw or Pruner**

These techniques can also be used, after the climber enters the tree, to advance or recrotch the climbing line to another location in the tree. This location is usually higher and more central in the tree, providing a more effective working position (pp. 56,58).

It is important for climbers to become proficient with all three techniques and determine which one is most suitable for the situation. It is a good practice to install a second line as well to be used as an access line for performing an aerial rescue in the event of an emergency. This line can also be used by the climber to work more efficiently in another part of the tree later on.

Installing ropes and climbing near electrical conductors is not for everyone!

Warning!

Climbing near electrical conductors is not for everyone! ANSI states "Only a qualified line-clearance tree trimmer or qualified line-clearance tree trimmer trainee shall be assigned to the work if it is found that an electrical hazard exists. A trainee shall be under the direct supervision of a qualified line-clearance tree trimmer."

When electrical or other potential hazards are present at or near the climbing site make certain that climbing lines are installed on the side of the tree away from them.

1. Throwline

The throwline has become the preferred method of rope installation. With the proper combination of throwline and throwbag (shot bag/pouch), accurate shots of 70 to 80 feet are possible with just a little practice. Installing a line high in the tree with the aid of a throwline is critical to provide positioning that enables the climber to work safely and efficiently. A high tie-in point will often eliminate the need to recrotch or advance the climbing line later.

The throwline is a simple yet versatile part of the climber's tool bag. It can be used to remove hangers and deadwood or to install a pull line in a tree to be felled. It is used to install and retrieve a false crotch or rope saver device and provide another means for a ground person to send equipment to the climber. The throwline is also commonly used while aloft to advance the climbing line later on and set a line in a neighboring tree.

Throwline Selection

There are several distinctive types of throwlines currently available to the climber. Factors to consider when selecting a throwline include the following: 1) line construction 2) breaking strength 3) weight and 4) surface tension/ friction (how slippery the line is). The latter two strongly influence how smoothly the throwline and bag can be manipulated in the tree and retrieved by the climber.

Perhaps the most popular throwline is constructed of 1/8 inch braided polyethylene or polypropylene (SlickLine). It is lightweight with a low surface tension allowing the throwline and bag to drop smoothly back to the ground. It does, however, have a low breaking strength. Nylon kernmantle cord of 1/8 inch diameter is preferred by those seeking a stronger and more flexible line that can be stuffed into a small line bag. It has a comparatively higher surface tension than polyethylene which may require a heavier throwbag to retrieve the line. Spectron 12 is another more specialized type of throwline. With a 1,200 pound breaking strength, this line is ideal for pulling down hangers and dead or broken limbs found during the tree inspection. Wrapping the throwline around a 12 inch stick serves as a sturdy handle when performing this type of operation.

The Throwbag

Throwbags are available in a variety of weights ranging from 12 to 20 ounces. Many factors must be considered when choosing the weight of the throwbag. Is the target crotch high or low in the tree? Is the throwline installed over a large diameter and/or rough barked limb? Does the throwline have a high or low surface tension? Lighter bags tend to throw higher while heavier bags allow for easier retrieval of heavy throwlines with high surface tension. Throwbags of 14 and 16 ounces are the most popular. Experiment with line and bag combinations to see what works best. Throwbags do get stuck, so keep several spares and extra lines on hand.

Throwing Procedure and Technique
Before using the throwline, the climbing site must be secure and the climber must be wearing head and eye protection. The throwline is "flaked" or piled end for end on the ground, or in a line bucket, bag, or tarp. This prevents the line from tangling and catching on twigs and other ground debris. Alert others with a verbal warning by shouting "stand clear!"

Two common techniques of throwing are the **single hand toss** (below left) and the **cradle throw** (below right). The single hand toss involves tying a slip knot in the line approximately three feet from the throwbag or with the bag on the ground at hip height. The knot acts as a grip for throwing which can easily be pulled or snapped out after the shot is made. The throwline is released during the forward motion of the swing.

The cradle throw consists of feeding a **bight** of throwline (a doubled section of line that doesn't cross itself) through the eye of the throwbag, centering it, and then throwing from between the legs. This method of configuring the throwline also works well with the single hand toss.

It's a good idea to keep the throwline within easy reach while making a shot. If it appears obvious the attempted shot is off target, the climber can stop the shot from going further, and potentially getting stuck, by simply stepping on or grabbing the throwline.

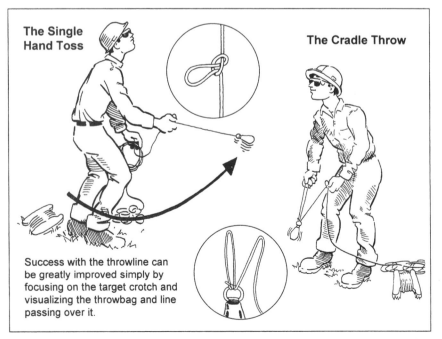

The Single Hand Toss

The Cradle Throw

Success with the throwline can be greatly improved simply by focusing on the target crotch and visualizing the throwbag and line passing over it.

Attaching the Throwline to the Throwbag

There are a variety of knots which can be used to attach the throwline to the ring of the throwbag. The Clove hitch, Anchor hitch, Bowline, and Figure Eight knot are all excellent choices. These knots are easy to tie, and they untie with varying degrees of ease, depending on the throwline material used.

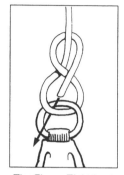

The Figure Eight knot

Many climbers attach a throwbag (usually heavier) on the other end of the throwline as well. This will prevent loosing the running end of the line after a shot has been made and provides a means of manipulating the line to isolate it around a single limb or tie-in point.

Attaching the Throwline to the Climbing Line

Once you make a successful shot attach the throwline to the climbing line using one of several methods. If the climbing line is being pulled through a narrow crotch or the rings of a false crotch, the throwbag will need to be removed and the throwline tied to the rope with two Clove hitches. This arrangement creates a streamlined effect facilitating installation. Half hitches can be added between the Clove hitches to lengthen the attachment.

Wide crotches are more forgiving, allowing for a single Clove hitch or Pile hitch to be tied down about a foot from the end of the rope. The Pile hitch is especially easy to untie after heavy jerking or loading has occurred on the rope. Perhaps the quickest method, if the crotch allows it, is to leave the throwbag on the throwline and pass the end of the climbing line through the eye of the throwbag, after which an Overhand knot is tied.

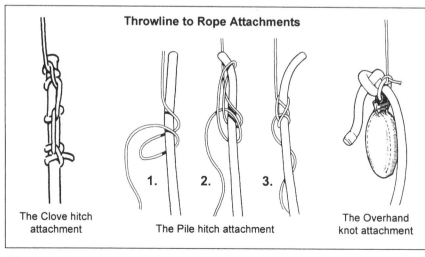

Throwline to Rope Attachments

1. 2. 3.

The Clove hitch attachment

The Pile hitch attachment

The Overhand knot attachment

Tools of the Trade: The Big Shot

The Big Shot is a throwline setting tool, introduced by Tobe Sherrill of Sherrill Arborist Supply, that enables users to accurately "fire" throwbags to heights in trees up to 80 feet or more. The Big Shot is a large offset slingshot that is designed to fit into the end of an eight foot fiberglass pruner pole.

The Big Shot is particularly useful for installing lines high in a tree with a dense canopy which limit and frustrate the effectiveness of hand thrown lines. Another virtue of the Big Shot is its ability to maintain a flat vertical trajectory. This enables the user to install lines while situated almost directly below the target crotch which is often necessary when working on sites that restrict and confine movement. It also proves valuable in areas with tall grass, deep snow, or dense understory that would otherwise interfere with hand throwing methods.

Before firing the Big Shot, take the same precautions as with hand thrown methods by wearing approved head and eye protection and ensuring the work site is safe. Place the throwbag in the pouch of the Big Shot with the pole firmly planted on the ground. The pouch is then pulled down using the fingerloops and released. Use a line bag, bucket, or tarp to keep the line from getting tangled or pile the line on a cleared area on the ground. Higher shots can be obtained using a rod and reel setup with lightweight Spectra line. Use this tool with caution because of its long firing range.

Making a long shot with the Big Shot.

Lowering the Throwline—Strumming

The throwline will often pass over and rub against several limbs and twigs before and/or after the target crotch. The friction this creates on the line inhibits
the throwbag from lowering properly to the ground. Occasionally a throwline
can be flipped back down. However, because of its comparatively light weight
it doesn't perform this task as well as rope does. "Strumming" is a technique
(sometimes referred to as the "bow and arrow" method) that provides remedy
to this situation, freeing the line so the end can be retrieved. Strumming is also
effective for releasing stuck throwbags. One method of strumming the line is
illustrated and described below.

1 Firmly grip the
throwline with one
outstretched hand.
With the other hand
apply tension on the
throwline by pinching
and pulling it back with
two fingers and the
thumb as if pulling back
the string on a bow.

2 Quickly release
or snap the
throwline. This will
send a wave of vibra-
tions along the line
releasing it and allow-
ing it to drop to the
ground. Several "shots"
or attempts may be
required to send the
bag down.

Isolating the Throwline—Single and Double Throwbag Technique

Once the throwline has been freed and is running smoothly in the tree it may
need to be manipulated so that the line is isolated around a single branch.
Eliminating other limbs can often be accomplished by simply pulling the
throwbag back up over and around interfering branches and to the target crotch
(but not over it). The throwbag is then manipulated by bouncing it into the desired position. If there are interfering limbs on both sides of the throwline a
throwbag attached to the other end of the line will need to be employed as
well. It is helpful if this bag is heavier than the primary throwbag (16-20
ounces). Like the first bag, the second is pulled up and over the interfering
limbs to the target crotch and then slowly manipulated back down so that both
legs of the throwline are plumb (straight down) and parallel to each other.

Isolating the Throwline—The Stick Trick

Sometimes the throwline has passed through the tree canopy in such a fashion that even the double throw-bag technique fails to yield the desired results. This is when the stick trick comes to the rescue. Performing the stick trick method as illustrated below usually works fine. However, in the event the throwline has passed over smaller diameter and smooth barked limbs, which have less friction on the line, a counter-weight may be necessary to prevent the climbing line from being pulled back down over the target crotch. In this event, form a bullet shaped throwing knot in the end of the rope with the rope snap exposed and then proceed as described below.

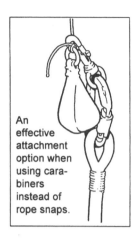

An effective attachment option when using cara-biners instead of rope snaps.

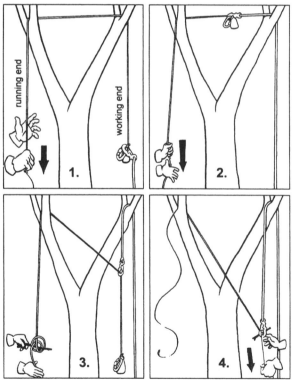

Helpful Hint: During step #3, tie the running end of line to the carabiner on the working end, to form a continuous loop. If the carabiner gets stuck, the climber can manipulate it through the tangle or retrieve it and start over.

1 Attach the climbing line, with attached rope snap, to the throwline just above the throwbag. Attach a carabiner through the throwbag ring to prevent the bag from getting stuck inside the rope snap opening.

2 Pull the rope snap and climbing line into the tree and just over the target crotch. Lower the throwbag back to the ground.

3 Secure a small stick or locking carabiner (non-locking types may open & become stuck) with a Clove hitch into the running end of the throwline.

4 Pull down on the working end of the throwline until the stick or carabiner catches the snap (or carabiner) and drag it back down.

25

Positioning the Rope—The Flip Stick

Even though the climber may successfully pull the climbing line over the desired limb, it may not be properly positioned in the crotch. For example, in the illustration below (Fig. a), the climbing line is away from the crotch just in front of a small sucker. For a more desirable position, the climbing line needs to be flipped into the crotch (Fig. c). If the line is relatively low in the tree, flipping the line can often be done by hand. The flip stick, however, is a trick that will enable the climber to send a larger loop of rope up into the tree than can be done by hand, especially when a line is set high in the tree. The flip stick can be a short stick or branch to which the climbing line is attached. (See the illustrations below.)

1 The climbing line is attached to the end of a 3-4 foot long stick with a Clove hitch. The climber holds the other end of the stick along with the remaining rope back over the shoulders.

2 Using a quick forward motion a large loop of rope is flipped into the tree over the branch toward the desired crotch (a). Several attempts are often necessary to walk the rope along the branch, possibly over small suckers (b), and back into the desired crotch (c).

 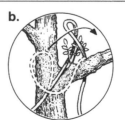 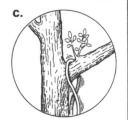

The "Flip Stick" technique allows the climber to "walk the rope" along the branch, over obstacles, and into the crotch.

Tools of the Trade: False Crotch Device

A false crotch is a device that provides an alternate route for a climbing line or rigging line to travel instead of passing over a natural crotch within the tree. This device goes by many names: cambium saver, rope saver, and Friction-Saver ™. Each title conveys in part some of the virtues of this popular tool. It protects the soft tissue layers of the limb (cambium) and the climbing line from damage caused from excessive friction that would otherwise occur from the rope passing and rubbing over the crotch of the tree. In this book the discussion of the device will be restricted to application for climbing lines, where it will be referred to as a "false crotch" device.

False Crotch Construction

False crotch devices most commonly consist of a nylon webbing strap with a large metal ring sewn into one end and a smaller ring sewn in the other. The rings are either aluminum or steel. Aluminum rings are light and dissipate heat well, while steel rings are stronger and more resistant to abrasion. Strap lengths range from two to six feet long. Larger trees necessitate the use of a longer strap. False crotches can also be made from rope or webbing slings.

Many climbers prefer using a false crotch device fitted with locking carabiners and screw links instead of closed rings. This option provides quick access for climbing systems rigged with attachment knots (vs. eye spliced ends) that first require untying before threading through the rings. This method allows for a further option of attaching a pulley (lower right) to decrease the bend radius of the rope and thereby further decrease friction and strength loss. Keep in mind, decreased friction at the tie-in point will increase friction at the friction hitch (see sidebar on p. 35). Regardless of how the false crotch is fashioned, the strength rating of the strap (or rope) and rings must match or exceed that required by ANSI for climbing lines and rope snaps.

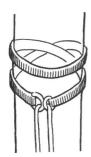

The false crotch can be wrapped around the trunk or stem where no natural crotch exists.

The false crotch is also a "moving crotch" that follows the climber's movements in the tree while providing consistent friction.

A false crotch rigged with carabiner, screw link, and small pulley.

27

Installing the False Crotch—While in the Tree

The false crotch can be installed while in the tree. Upon reaching the desired tie-in point place the device in a suitable crotch or wrap it once around the trunk or stem, where no crotch exists (p. 27, lower left). The latter method requires the device be long enough to allow the rings to come together in front. Next, pass the working end of the climbing line through both rings of the device and tie in. Whenever possible, avoid placing this device in tight crotches.

Installing the False Crotch—From the Ground: Method 1

1 Install and isolate the throwline around the crotch. Pass the running end through the large ring and the working end (end with throwbag) through the small ring. The throwbag will need to be removed first and then reattached afterward. If the ring of the throwbag slips through the ring of the false crotch, attach a carabiner to the throwbag ring (see step #1, p. 29). Raise the false crotch into the tree by pulling on the throwline.

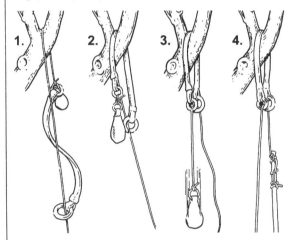

2 Pull on the throwline until the device just reaches the crotch. Give a quick yank and the device will flip it into position in the crotch.

3 Lower the throwbag and line back to the ground.

4 Secure the throwline to the rope with two clove hitches (Half hitch in between is optional) and pull through the rings and back to ground.

Retrieving the False Crotch

1 Tie an Overhand or Figure Eight knot in the rope end that will pass through the large ring first. The knot must be small enough to fit through the large ring but large enough to catch on the smaller ring.

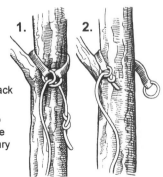

2 Continue pulling the rope as the knot catches the smaller ring of the device allowing it to be pulled back to the ground.

It is strongly recommended that a throwline be tied to the rope to control the descent of the false crotch device during retrieval. This will protect the user from head injury and the false crotch from damage caused from ground impact. This will also prevent hang-ups in the tree.

Installing the False Crotch—From the Ground: Method 2

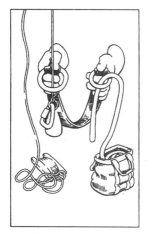

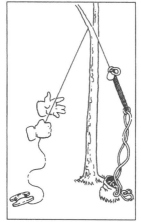

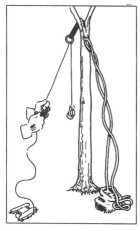

1 Insert throwbag through large ring of false crotch. Attach a carabiner to the throwbag. Run the climbing line though the small ring.

2 Pull the running end of the throwline and raise the device into the crotch. Both ends of the climbing line must remain on the ground during this process.

3 After the false crotch device is in position, lower the throwbag with attached carabiner to the ground.

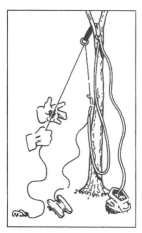

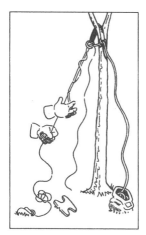

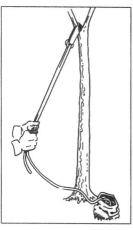

4 At this point, make certain to attach the *correct* end of the throwline to the *correct* end of the climbing line or the entire rig may get locked into position.

5 Pull down on the throwline so the climbing line passes through the large ring and comes back to the ground.

6 The false crotch is now properly installed and ready to go to work.

Tools of the Trade: Rope Saver

The rope saver is a leather horseshoe-shaped tool that, like the false crotch device, protects the climbing line and tree limb from abrasion and heat damage caused from excessive friction. It also protects the rope from pitchy conifer trees. Since the rope saver assumes the shape and size of the crotch, the climbing line maintains a larger radius than when placed through the two rings of the false crotch device, thereby retaining rope strength. This device can also be used on lowering lines when performing lightweight rigging operations through a natural crotch.

Installing the Rope Saver

Begin by straightening the rope saver as much as possible and threading the climbing line through with a twisting motion. If the device will be installed from the ground using a throwline, follow the procedure in the drawings below. If the climber will install the device while in the tree at the tie-in point, pre-rig a climbing system, such as the split-tail system, for a quick tie in. This will enable the climber to simply plop the device into a suitable crotch without having to rig the system while aloft.

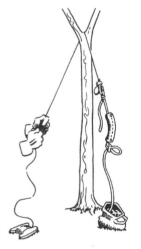 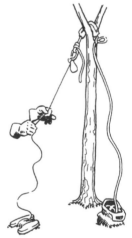 

1 Attach one end of the climbing line to the throwline (with or without attached connecting device). Tie a Slip knot just behind the rope saver.

2 Pull the rope saver up to the crotch. The Slip knot will assist in pushing the rope saver into position.

3 Pull hard on the rope while holding the throwline taut to release the knot. Continue pulling the throwline until the rope end can be reached.

Retrieving the Rope Saver

Tie an Overhand knot in one end of the climbing line and pull down on the other end. The knot will catch on the rope saver and dislodge it from the crotch. Although the rope saver is less likely than the false crotch to get stuck in the tree, a throwline may be used to control the descent, just in case.

2. Throwing Knot

A throwing knot is nothing more than a throwing weight fashioned out of the end of the rope. A series of coils and wraps holds the knot together and provides the end-weight necessary for throwing, flipping, and retrieving. The knot may be tied around the rope snap to provide additional weight. Before the throwline gained popularity, the throwing knot was the standard method of rope installation. With practice, the throwing knot can be very effective in reaching heights up to about 40 feet or more.

If the knot is tied in the **open form** (when the climber is reasonably certain of making the shot the first time) it will unwind down toward the climber after the shot is made. In the **closed form**, a bight of rope is looped over the entire knot preventing it from unraveling.

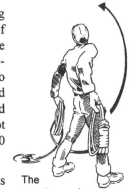

The rope toss using "sidearm" technique. Other methods include the underhand and over the head.

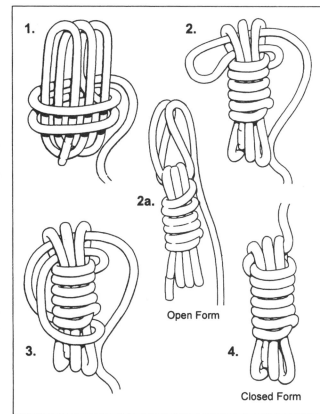

1.

2.

2a.

Open Form

3.

4.

Closed Form

1 Start by making three or four small loops of rope followed by the desired number of round turns around the loops (4-7).

2 After the last turn place a bight of rope through the loops. This can serve as a handle when throwing in the *open form* (Fig. 2a).

3 To make the *closed form* (Fig. 4) continue passing the bight of rope down and around the entire throwing knot, removing all the slack, to lock the knot.

4 The finished knot should be tight, compact and, when tied properly, a work of art. The knot can be made heavier by adding wraps and loops.

The Noose Knot

Another type of throwing knot that has some very unique characteristics is the Noose knot. As the name implies, the Noose knot is actually a Hangman's knot with the noose end closed and partially tucked into the coils. The Noose knot provides an excellent alternative for climbers who always manage to get the traditional throwing knot stuck. A steady pull on the running end of a Noose knot wedged in a tight crotch will unravel and free itself from what otherwise could have been a frustrating and inconvenient situation.

In addition, with practice, this knot is faster to make than the traditional throwing knot and assumes a more streamlined, missile-like shape. Historically the knot was tied with an odd number of turns (seven minimum, thirteen maximum). Leave enough of the noose sticking out from the end to prevent the top turn from rolling off the end and unraveling the knot.

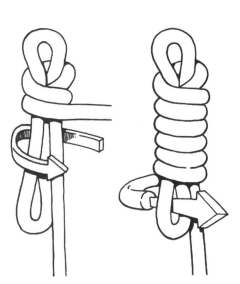

1 Near the end of the rope close a bight leaving a long tail (3-4 feet). Make a second bight and make a series of downward turns around the loops.

2 Tighten the turns well, one at a time, and pass the end through the eye of the lower bight.

3 Tighten the bottom eye snugly around the end by pulling the left side of the top eye.

4 Pull on the tail to draw all but about one inch of the top eye into the coils.

3. Pole Saw or Pruner

The pole saw or pruner provides an effective means of installing a climbing line from the ground when the tree has low branches. Typically, the climber ties a variation of the throwing knot which is looped over the hook opposite the blade or pruner head. The rope is then dropped over the target crotch and pulled back down to the climber with the hook end of the saw or pruner. Be sure to keep the rope away from the cutting portion of the saw or pruner head. It is a good idea to inspect the rope for cuts after each use with a pole saw or pruner. Some climbers use a pole saw with the scabbard left on or with the blade removed when setting ropes.

Keep the rope away from the cutting portion of the pole saw or pruner head.

Once the climber has entered the tree, the pole saw or pruner can be used to advance or reposition the climbing line higher or into a better position (p. 56). The climber must be secured in the tree with a personal lanyard when performing this operation. The pole saw is also an excellent tool for removing deadwood and hangers found along the climbing path which pose as a potential hazard for the climber or ground person. It's a good idea to have extra saw blades, and attachment nuts and bolts in the tool box.

Tip of the Trade: Rope Placement

Avoid installing the climbing line over the lowest branch in the tree. Instead, select a suitable crotch or branch that is located above another one, large and sturdy enough to provide a "landing" for the climber to step onto after reaching the tie-in point. From this position the climber will be able to safely and comfortably "clip-in" with a lanyard and tie in to a climbing system or advance the climbing line. It is extremely awkward and tiring to maneuver from the underside of a branch, without a foothold beneath it, to a position of security on top.

E—Entering the Tree

Tree climbers have a variety of techniques to choose when entering the tree—the third step of the P.R.E.P. system. Each entry technique discussed in this section of the book has a specific application. The most versatile climbers become familiar and proficient with all six entry techniques. This enables them to choose a technique that best suits the situation at hand, thereby maximizing the climber's performance and productivity. The techniques for entering the tree include the following:

1. **Ladders**
2. **Alternate Lanyard Technique (ALT)**
3. **Body Thrusting**
4. **Secured Footlock**
5. **Single Rope Technique (SRT)**
6. **Climbing Spurs**

The entry techniques listed above are often used in combination. For instance, climbers may enter the lower tree canopy using a ladder and then continue their ascent to a tie-in point higher in the tree using the alternate lanyard technique. Generally, the secured footlock and single rope technique are used for canopy

The "Low and Slow" Rule

Practice new climbing techniques "low and slow"—low in the tree and slowly integrated into practice. Master each technique before a new one is added.

access only and replaced with a dynamic climbing line system afterward. This system is much more efficient when climbing and performing work aloft.

Regardless of entry technique, the climber typically will want to perform some tree work while making vertical progress in the tree. This is usually limited to the removal of dead limbs and hangers found along the path of the climbing line. The climber must have two means of securing his or her position aloft.

Tree Inspection Revisited

The climber's view of the tree changes the moment he or she "saddles up" and begins ascending. Objects and hazards within the canopy, which were not visible from the ground, come into view. The same attentiveness necessary to perform the pre-climb inspection from the ground, must also be employed while climbing and working aloft. If a hazard is detected while ascending, the climber may have to reconsider the climbing route and work plan, or decide against climbing the tree at all. One option climbers may consider is to tie in to a backup climbing system installed in a neighboring tree (p. 50). This method is particularly useful when performing hazardous tree removals.

Dynamic and Static Climbing Line Systems

The entry techniques which require the use of a climbing line can be divided into two types of systems—the **dynamic** and **static** climbing line systems. These terms describe the action of the climbing line while it is being employed to enter and work in the tree.

With a dynamic climbing line system, the rope moves with the climber as he or she moves and works in the tree. The body thrust technique employs this type of system. When the climber pulls down on the running end of the line the working end moves upward—with the climber. The climber's progress is secured, or "captured" by sliding the friction hitch along the running end of the climbing line. When used for this purpose, the friction hitch provides a **self belay** enabling the climber to easily alternate between ascending and descending. For this reason, a dynamic climbing line system is usually preferred by climbers as the primary means of working in the tree.

With a static line system, the climber ascends a fixed or stationary rope. The secured footlock and single rope technique utilize this type of system. Climbers use friction hitches, ascenders, and/or feet to ascend the rope and secure their position while climbing and working. A separate device is installed when performing a descent from the tree and is used in combination with the friction hitch which serves as a self belay. The static line system is preferred by many climbers as a means of canopy access. It is often chosen for long ascents and/or when the rope cannot be isolated around a single limb.

Friction—Friend or Foe?

Whenever a climbing or rigging line moves across an object, friction occurs. This action is most evident when using a dynamic climbing line system and the rope rubs across the bark of a natural crotch, the surface of a rope saver, or through the rings of a false crotch. The friction that occurs between the rope and a natural crotch, for instance, can be a good thing for the climber performing the body thrust technique, since it helps to hold his or her position until the friction hitch can be advanced. More friction at the tie-in point also means less friction at the friction hitch. This too is good. However, this may not be such a good thing for the crotch of thin barked trees or the rope passing over it since the abrasion and heat created from the friction can potentially damage both.

False crotch and rope saver devices provide a partial solution to the latter dilemma. They radically reduce wear and tear on the rope and tree crotch by decreasing friction at the tie-in point. The tradeoff of this effect however, is displaced friction or, in this case, an increase in friction at the friction hitch. This means the hitch may tighten up more readily and burn out sooner. This threat can be significantly reduced by simply performing slow and controlled descents and inspecting rope ends and split tails often, replacing them when necessary. While descending, check and feel the hitch—if it is warm, slow down or stop and let it cool off.

---

1. Ladders

Ladders provide a quick and easy means of entering the tree when branches are low enough to permit their use. The safest method to enter the tree with a ladder is to install a climbing line and tie in with an approved friction hitch with micro pulley (p. 55). Finally, have a second person belay the climber by holding down on the climbing line. This will cause the micro pulley to advance the friction hitch. If desired, the climber may perform a self belay on the line.

Climber is secured with climbing line while second worker steadies the ladder.

Proper ladder angle

It has also been customary for a climber to free climb the ladder and secure his or her position with a lanyard when a suitable tie-in point is reached. A climbing line is then installed using one of the rope installation/advance methods. A second worker steadies the ladder during the climb. The climber must always be tied in with either a climbing line or lanyard when performing work from a ladder.

Ladder Safety

1. A second worker should support the ladder from below while the climber ascends. Remove the ladder when the climber is in the tree to avoid damage from dropped limbs.

2. A ladder will sometimes be more secure when positioned against a side branch instead of the main trunk where it tends to rock back and forth on the top rung. Avoid cutting the limb supporting the ladder!

3. Do not carry tools or materials in your hand while climbing the ladder. Use a tool pouch or have a ground person send them up later.

4. Ladders made of metal or other conductive material must not be used where an electrical hazard exists.

Proper Ladder Setup

1 Set the ladder into position. Secure the locks on extension ladders.

2 While standing erect, place toes against the side rails at the bottom of the ladder.

3 With arms extended straight out and parallel to the ground, the hands should just be able to reach the backside of the ladder.

2. Alternate Lanyard Technique (ALT)

In smaller trees, or trees that have low and closely spaced branches, the climber may choose to enter the tree using the alternate lanyard technique or ALT. This technique involves the alternating use of two personal lanyards (hence the name) while the climber advances his or her position in the tree by using the limbs and trunk for hand and foot holds.

It is important that the climber maintain three points of contact with the tree while climbing. In addition, limbs should be tested before the climber commits weight on them. If possible, dead and broken branches should be removed as they are encountered.

To perform the ALT, the climber begins ascending the tree while secured with a personal lanyard. When a limb is encountered the second lanyard is employed by passing one end above the limb and back to the climber's saddle. At this point the climber releases the first lanyard and proceeds up the tree until another limb or obstacle is encountered.

This process is repeated, alternating between lanyards, until the desired tie-in point is reached. It is absolutely necessary for the climber to be secured to the tree at all times.

The 2-in-1 or doubled-end lanyard is an excellent choice when using the ALT. This lanyard has a rope snap or carabiner on each end (p. 38). The climber alternates tying in with the ends of the lanyard instead of alternating between two separate lanyards. The lanyard length is adjusted with a Prusik knot, which, by its symmetrical configuration, grabs the lanyard when loaded from either direction.

A more versatile option yet, is to use a split-tail climbing system as a second lanyard. The range of adjustment is as long as the rope, and when equipped with a micro pulley, the length can be adjusted with one hand. In addition, the split-tail climbing system enables the climber to perform a quick tie in when a suitable crotch is reached.

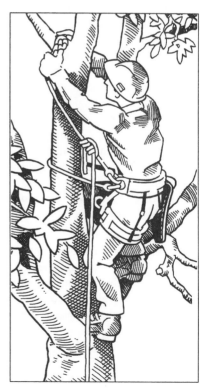

This climber is using a split-tail climbing system as a second lanyard for secured positioning while passing a limb.

37

Tools of the Trade: Lanyards

Next to the climbing line, a lanyard is the climber's most important tool for securing his or her position while climbing and working in the tree. Lanyards that perform this function are referred to as personal, safety, or work positioning lanyards.

Lanyards consist of three main components: the lanyard itself (rope construction), connecting devices (carabiners, rope snaps, or screw links), and the lanyard adjuster. There are a variety of lanyard types available and combinations by which the lanyard components can be assembled. Several of the most commonly used types of lanyards are discussed below.

Hip Prusik Lanyards

This type of lanyard utilizes a Prusik loop as the lanyard adjuster. It is tied to the lanyard with a Prusik loop and clipped-in to the side D-ring of the climber's saddle. When a micro pulley is attached to the lanyard below the friction hitch, one-handed length adjustment is possible. Another nice feature of the hip Prusik lanyard is that both ends may be used making it a 2-in-1 or double-ended lanyard, since the Prusik knot will grip when loaded from either direction. This is particularly useful when climbing with the alternate lanyard technique. *In order for the 2-in-1 lanyard to function properly, the micro pulley must be removed.*

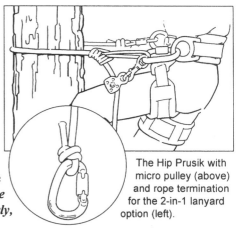

The Hip Prusik with micro pulley (above) and rope termination for the 2-in-1 lanyard option (left).

Camming Lanyards

Camming lanyards employ the use of a cammed ascender (p. 47) to adjust lanyard length. This method also allows for one-handed lanyard adjustment. Cammed ascenders, however, are designed to be loaded from one direction only, and are therefore not safe for use as a 2-in-1 lanyard. Replace the pin that comes with many cammed ascenders with a lock nut and bolt.

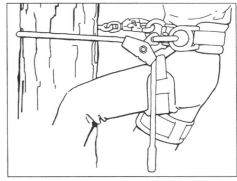

Camming lanyards provide one-handed length adjustment (not to be used as a 2-in-1 lanyard).

Wire Core Lanyards

This type of lanyard is also referred to as a "flipline" and is commonly used when performing tree removal operations. The wire core, which is housed inside a rope body, is stiff enough to facilitate easy flipping of the line up the trunk of the tree as well as provide some protection when operating a hand saw or chainsaw.

Regardless of lanyard type, it is strongly recommended that climbers use two means attachment when operating a chain saw in the tree. Wire core lanyards can be adjusted using a hip Prusik with

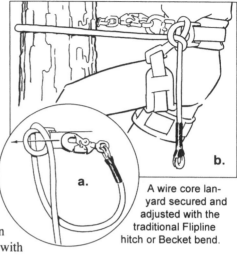

b.

A wire core lanyard secured and adjusted with the traditional Flipline hitch or Becket bend.

micro pulley, a cammed ascender, or the traditional Flipline hitch (Fig. a,b). *A wire core lanyard must never be used near energized conductors!*

Split-Tail Lanyards

The climbing line becomes an exceptional second or backup lanyard when rigged with the split-tail climbing system (p. 53). Frequently, climbers bring their climbing line along during the ascent anyway, to be used after reaching the canopy. Therefore, it makes good sense to employ it as a second lanyard as well. Split-tail lanyards are as long as the rope and when assembled with a micro pulley, allow for one handed length adjustment. Using a split tail as a lanyard is a very effective way of passing limbs when using the alternate lanyard technique. In addition, the split tail is ready to be installed as a climbing system the moment a suitable tie-in point is reached. This can be a real comfort (lifesaver) during an unexpected encounter with an active hornets nest.

Making Your Own Lanyards

Climbers frequently construct their own lanyards to fit their particular climbing needs. Three-strand rope has been the standard for making lanyards for years. It's inexpensive, easy to eye splice, and is stiff enough to flip easily. Another popular option is 16-strand climbing line. An approved connecting device is secured to one end of the lanyard (or both with a 2-in-1 lanyard) with a suitable attachment knot or eye splice. Another connecting device attaches the lanyard adjuster to the climber's saddle. A protective sheath for the lanyard can be made by passing the rope through a length of 2-inch tubular webbing before attaching the connecting device. All lanyard components—rope, connecting device, and lanyard adjuster must meet ANSI strength standards.

1 The climber starts by placing feet high on the trunk.

Working end

Running end

Pull
Down

2 The climber thrusts the hips forward while pulling down hard with the arms.

Slide
Up

3 The friction hitch is then quickly advanced to take up rope slack.

3. Body Thrusting

Body thrusting utilizes a dynamic climbing line system. It is used most often when the installed climbing line lies against or near the tree.

The "classic" body thrust technique begins with the climber "tying in" to the working end of the climbing line using an approved attachment knot and leaving a 3-4 foot tail (See: traditional climbing system, p. 53.) The tail is used to tie a suitable friction hitch to the running end of the climbing line thus forming the "bridge"—the length of rope between the attachment knot and the friction hitch. A long bridge is recommended with this technique in order to achieve optimal performance. However, climbers will need to experiment to determine the bridge length that works best for them.

As the drawings demonstrate, the climber places the feet high on the tree trunk and thrusts the hips forward while simultaneously pulling down on the rope just below the friction hitch. The climber quickly slides the friction hitch forward, to take up the slack in the rope.

The friction that is created between the rope and the natural crotch in the tree helps to hold the climber's position until the friction hitch can be advanced. The climber repeats these motions, literally walking up the trunk of the tree, until the destination is reached. If the climber decides to descend or move to a position lower in the tree, the process is simply reversed by sliding the friction hitch downward or toward the climber. (The proper procedure for belaying a climber while body thrusting is on page 55; descending procedure is on page 64.)

Modified Body Thrust

The modified body thrust technique enhances the effectiveness of body thrusting by incorporating the energy saving features of the footlock technique—principally the large leg muscles (pp. 42-43). This technique is particularly useful when the climbing line is situated away from the trunk and limbs when the climber has descended part way down the tree (while performing work operations) and then wishes to return to his or her original position.

The modified body thrust begins with the climber rocking backward from a sitting position and taking up the rope with both feet below the friction hitch, one foot on top of the other, forming a lock on the rope. The climber stands up on the footlock and advances the friction hitch. This technique is also referred to as "footlocking the tail."

There are several other options available for "grabbing the tail" of the climbing line with something other than the climber's feet. A Prusik loop tied to the rope below the friction hitch serves as a foot loop that the climber can stand up on. This technique is well suited for beginning and young climbers who may not yet have developed much upper body strength. In fact, any "rope grab" device (p. 46) or technique designed for ascending a single line will work equally well with the modified body thrust.

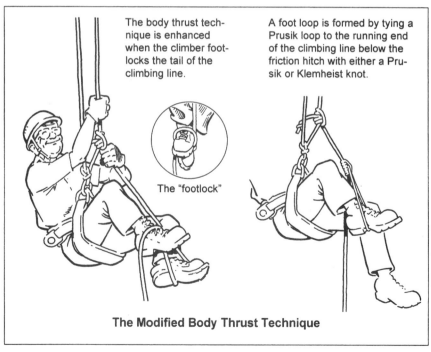

The body thrust technique is enhanced when the climber footlocks the tail of the climbing line.

A foot loop is formed by tying a Prusik loop to the running end of the climbing line below the friction hitch with either a Prusik or Klemheist knot.

The "footlock"

The Modified Body Thrust Technique

4. Secured Footlock

The secured footlock technique is often selected when the climbing line is suspended in the tree away from the trunk, making body thrusting a difficult and fatiguing option. Footlocking incorporates the strongest muscles of the climber—the legs, thereby making this a real energy saving technique. This technique is a classic example of a static line system (stationary) that is used by climbers primarily as a means of access only.

Although footlocking a static line(s) provides an efficient means of entering the tree, climbers are limited in their ability to move or work within the canopy. Unless the work to be performed in the tree is close to the path of the climbing line, climbers must tie in to a dynamic climbing line system that allows a greater range of mobility. Climbers who choose to stay tied in to the static line system need to incorporate the use of approved descending equipment and techniques before leaving the tree (p. 64-65).

1 The climber begins by tying the Prusik loop to the doubled climbing line with three wraps (six coils) of either a Prusik or a Klemheist knot. The other end is attached to the climber's saddle using a double-locking carabiner or rope snap.

2 The climber grabs both ropes with hands below the friction hitch. The rope is placed against the outside of one foot.

3 As the legs are raised, *both* strands of the rope are scooped up with the opposite or lower foot.

4 The rope is then gripped securely between the feet with a wrap around one boot, forming the "footlock."

5 As the climber stands, the Prusik loop is advanced and the process repeated.

Handled ascenders may also be used as a means of attachment on the doubled climbing line (p. 47).

The Prusik Loop

As climbers ascend the doubled climbing line, their progress is "captured" with the method by which they are secured or tied in to the line. One method of tying in uses the Prusik loop. The Prusik loop is formed by joining the ends of a cord, which meet ANSI strength standards for climbing lines, using a Double Fisherman's knot or the Sliding Double Fisherman's knot. The length of cord needed to form a 4-6 foot long loop will be almost 12 feet long. It is important that the diameter of the Prusik cord be less than the diameter of the climbing line. Prusik loops constructed of 5/16 to 3/8 inch diameter cord are optimal when climbing a doubled 1/2 inch diameter line (1 inch combined).

The Friction Hitch

Two very effective friction hitches for securing the Prusik loop to the climbing line is the Prusik and the Klemheist knot. Each knot functions basically the same. When the climber's weight (load) is applied to the Prusik loop, the knot "grabs" the rope thereby securing the climber's position. When the load is relieved the knot can be loosened, enabling it to be raised or lowered. To be effective, the Prusik cord is tied onto the climbing line with a minimum of three wraps or six coils, regardless of knot choice. Finally, the end of the Prusik loop is secured to the central anchor point of the climbing saddle by an approved double-locking carabiner or rope snap.

Prusik Loop Precautions

As effective as the Prusik loop is for securing the climber to the climbing line, it has limitations. It is critical for climbers to understand what they are and what precautions should be taken to avoid trouble.

1. **Tie, dress, and set:** The friction hitch will not grab the rope or secure the climber properly unless the knot has been tied, dressed, and set properly.

2. **Hands below the knot:** When ascending it is important to keep both hands below the friction hitch to avoid accidentally disabling it, causing a rapid and uncontrolled descent. Make sure the Prusik loop is long enough.

3. **Ascent only:** The Prusik loop is intended for ascending only! It is only used as part of a descending system when combined with a figure-8 or similar descending device where it functions as a self belay.

4. **Debris out of the knot:** Keep leaves, twigs, and debris out of the friction hitch or it could fail. Remove debris immediately!

5. **Spread in the rope:** As the climber approaches the tie-in point, the spread in the rope increases relative to the branch diameter. Climbers should keep their Prusik loop and knot a reasonable distance away for this rope spread (five inches for every one inch of limb diameter—a 1:5 ratio) or the wraps of the knot may be forced open leading to knot failure.

5. Single Rope Technique (SRT)

The single rope technique (SRT) also employs a static climbing line system and is used as a means of canopy access only. The SRT is hard to beat when the climb is long or when the rope cannot be isolated around a single limb. This is often the case when installing lines in tall conifers or thickly crowned deciduous trees. Many of the same working and descending limitations that exist when footlocking on a doubled line apply to the SRT as well.

The suggested equipment, procedures, and techniques presented on the following pages are but a few of many options available for climbing a single line. For more information on SRT see the book *On Rope,* by Smith/Padgett.

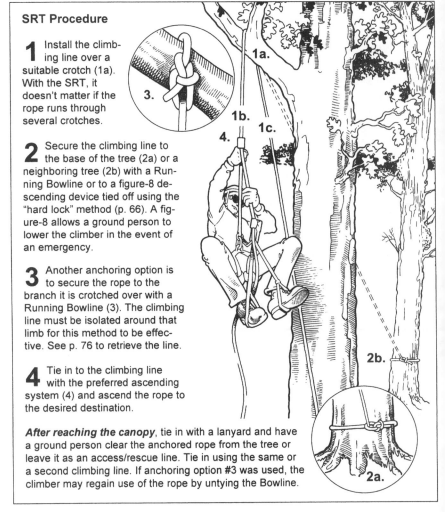

SRT Procedure

1 Install the climbing line over a suitable crotch (1a). With the SRT, it doesn't matter if the rope runs through several crotches.

2 Secure the climbing line to the base of the tree (2a) or a neighboring tree (2b) with a Running Bowline or to a figure-8 descending device tied off using the "hard lock" method (p. 66). A figure-8 allows a ground person to lower the climber in the event of an emergency.

3 Another anchoring option is to secure the rope to the branch it is crotched over with a Running Bowline (3). The climbing line must be isolated around that limb for this method to be effective. See p. 76 to retrieve the line.

4 Tie in to the climbing line with the preferred ascending system (4) and ascend the rope to the desired destination.

After reaching the canopy, tie in with a lanyard and have a ground person clear the anchored rope from the tree or leave it as an access/rescue line. Tie in using the same or a second climbing line. If anchoring option #3 was used, the climber may regain use of the rope by untying the Bowline.

Climbing Line Anchoring Precautions

There are concerns and potential hazards that exist when the climbing line is anchored to the base of the tree that do not occur when anchoring the line to the limb itself. Climbers need to be aware of the loading forces that occur on the branch or crotch that is *redirecting* the climbing line (1a) to an anchor point below (2a, 2b). This situation exposes the redirecting limb to twice the load that would occur if the rope was *anchored* to the branch itself (3).

For example, if the climber weighs 200 pounds, that means 200 pounds will be on the load "leg" of the climbing line (1b) and 200 pounds on the tension leg (1c). This exerts a total of 400 pounds of static load on the limb redirecting the rope (1a). It is critical therefore, that the tie-in point selected is strong enough to support this increased load.

Secondly, the climber must take precautions against cutting the tension "leg" of the climbing line (1c) with a hand saw or chainsaw. Many SRT climbers avoid this potential entirely by reserving use of the climbing line as a means of access only. Work is only performed after tying in to a more suitable climbing system. If it is necessary to perform limited work with any type of saw during the ascent the risk of cutting the line can be greatly reduced by using brightly colored rope (for better visibility) and anchoring the line in such a way that it is in full view. *In addition, it is imperative that the climber tie in with a second means of attachment when operating the saw!*

Selecting an Ascending System

The single rope climber has a variety of equipment and ascending systems from which to choose, each one offering a different level of efficiency and safety. There is, quite literally, a climbing system suitable for anyone, regardless of age, weight, or strength. For these reasons, the SRT is the preferred method with recreational tree climbers and becoming increasingly popular with professional tree climbers as well. Experience is the best teacher in determining which ascending system best meets the climber's needs. There are however, certain criteria to help the climber make that selection and design an ascending system. The system, along with its components should:

1.   ... grab the rope securely and allow for easy upward movement.

2.   ... allow the climber to use the major muscle groups for most of the effort.

3.   ... enable the climber to stop while enroute to rest or perform limited work operations.

4.   ... provide at least two attachment points for means of ascension, as well as fall protection, to secure the climber's position in the event that one point fails. The "sit-stand" method (p. 46) satisfies these requirements.

SRT Ascending Options

All SRT ascending systems incorporate at least two attachment points on the rope by which the climber alternates weight transfer. These attachment points are commonly referred to as "rope grab" devices, such as mechanical ascenders and friction hitches, or techniques, such as footlocking. When the climber's weight is applied to one rope grab, it becomes possible to advance the other one, thereby advancing the climber's position as well. However, not all rope grab or attachment point options provide fall protection (e.g., footlocking, foot loop). In those cases it is strongly recommended that the climber add an additional point of attachment that does. Illustrated below is the popular "sit-stand" method (which provides two means of fall protection) and several rope grab options which create a combination of at least two points of attachment.

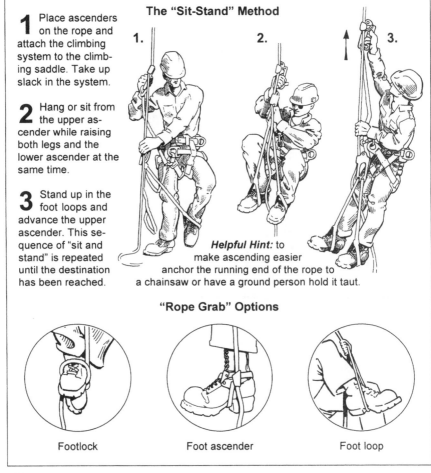

1 Place ascenders on the rope and attach the climbing system to the climbing saddle. Take up slack in the system.

2 Hang or sit from the upper ascender while raising both legs and the lower ascender at the same time.

3 Stand up in the foot loops and advance the upper ascender. This sequence of "sit and stand" is repeated until the destination has been reached.

The "Sit-Stand" Method

1.   2.   3.

Helpful Hint: to make ascending easier anchor the running end of the rope to a chainsaw or have a ground person hold it taut.

"Rope Grab" Options

Footlock   Foot ascender   Foot loop

Tools of the Trade: Ascenders

Ascenders are a rope grab device that have found favor among tree climbers because of their efficiency and versatility. There are two main groups of ascenders: **cammed** and **toothed**.

Cammed Ascenders

The most commonly used cammed ascenders (Gibbs, Macrograb, Microcender) consist of a shell that houses a grooved cam which, when activated, grips the enclosed rope. Cammed ascenders are commonly employed as lanyard adjusters. Some types of ascenders are well suited for fashioning a foot ascender providing an outstanding means for hands free ascending on a single line. Another type of camming device, referred to as the **"Footlocker,"** consists of a pair of cams combined in a single shell, providing a self belay when footlocking a doubled climbing line.

Paired ascenders secure the climber to the rope while footlocking.

Toothed Ascenders

Toothed ascenders rely on small spike-like teeth on a moving cam to provide the grip on the rope. Some designs have handles to grip and operate the device. Handled ascenders have become standard equipment for the SRT and when climbing a doubled line while footlocking. The pre-drilled holes in the shell allow for joining two ascenders together (for climbing a doubled line) and attaching footloops, slings, and straps.

Ascender Precautions

1. **Accidental opening:** Keep leaves, twigs, and debris out of and away from the spring and camming mechanism to prevent accidental opening. The climber's hands should be below the camming device during the ascent.

2. **Removing ascenders from the rope:** When removing toothed ascenders from the rope, take care to prevent the teeth from "picking" and pulling out the rope fibers. By design, the cams on the ascender can only be opened after the load has been relieved.

3. **Ascender backup:** Some ascenders require a backup means of fall protection. Doubled ascenders, for instance, do not provide twice the protection when used in the manner illustrated above. If one ascender fails, the entire system fails. One method of backing up ascenders entails tying a Prusik loop above the ascender with a friction hitch. The loop is secured to the climber's saddle with a carabiner. This arrangement enables the ascender to advance the friction hitch as it is raised. If the cams on the ascenders open or fail to grip the rope, the Prusik loop will provide fall protection.

6. Climbing Spurs

Climbing spurs provide an efficient means of entering the tree but are a valid choice *only* when climbing and working in trees that are to be removed. The only exception to this is in the event of an emergency to expedite an aerial rescue. These limitations are due to the potential for causing injury to the tree from wounds left by the gaffs, or spurs, particularly on thin barked trees.

The climbing spur, as a unit, is referred to as a "climber" and consists of several components: the stirrup, shank, lower strap, gaff, pads, and upper straps. For climbing spurs to function effectively it is important that they are inspected daily, sized and fastened properly, and that the gaffs are kept sharp.

Work boots used with spurs should have a reinforced shank to protect the arch of the foot. Boots with the traditional "loggers heel" work well for holding the stirrup in place. However, flat-soled boots can be worn when the lower strap of the "climber" is wrapped once around the shank before fastening.

Double wrapping the lanyard

Climbing Tips

1. Set gaffs firmly into the tree at a distance apart no more than the width of your shoulders.

2. Step up on the stirrups and lock or slightly bend the knee. Repeat the process with the other leg. Alternate steps as you would when climbing a ladder.

3. Take short steps while learning, advancing the lanyard between steps. As skill improves, longer steps can be taken. Reverse this procedure when climbing down.

4. Keep the lanyard as horizontal to your climbing saddle as possible.

5. Place hands on the lanyard near the trunk to advance—watch the fingers and wear gloves.

6. Climb the backside of the tree, taking advantage of the lean.

7. Prevent gaff "kick-out" by maintaining a gaff angle of about 45°, avoiding sheets of loose bark, and having sharp gaffs.

8. When in a stationary position, lock one knee to relieve leg and foot fatique.

9. Double-wrap the lanyard to create a choker effect which will more effectively secure the climber's position.

Climbing Secured with Lanyards and Climbing Line
Climbers must be secured at all times while climbing with spurs by using either a lanyard (flipline) or climbing line. When climbing past limbs encountered along the way, it will be necessary for climbers to have a second means of securing their position as well. It is strongly recommended that the second means of security also be employed when operating a chain saw in the tree, thereby doubling the margin of safety. The procedure for passing limbs or obstacles using two lanyards is the same as the alternate lanyard technique.

Perhaps the most versatile and important tool to take along while climbing with spurs is a climbing line, especially one pre-rigged with the multi-purpose split-tail system (p. 53). The climbing line provides a link between the ground worker and the climber—a means of exchanging tools, for instance. It is used to access the limbs to be rigged for removal and offers a means of escape from bees and hornets, etc. The split-tail system can also function as a second lanyard with a range of adjustment as long as the rope.

One method of using the split-tail system as a second lanyard is to "choker" it around the main stem. This will more effectively secure the climber's position if a "kick-out" occurs or if climbers wish to support their weight on the rope to relieve foot and leg pressure. This method is especially useful when climbing smooth barked trees or when the stem diameter decreases as the climber ascends.

To rig the split tail in this fashion, pass the working end of the climbing line around the trunk and clip the carabiner or rope snap onto the climbing line above the friction hitch. A Running Bowline will also accomplish this same effect. Next, move the working end of the split tail from the side D-ring to the central tie-in point on the saddle, and advance the friction hitch as close to the choker as possible. As the climber applies weight to the system, the rope will tighten. A similar effect can be created by double wrapping the primary lanyard around the tree (see opposite page). The primary and the split-tail lanyard are advanced at the same time by first loosening and opening the choker and then gripping them together. Be careful not to gaff into the rope while climbing! *Do not descend solely on the friction hitch; instead use a figure-8 descender.* By attaching a throwline (or rope end) to the carabiner of the chokered split-tail system, the climber can retrieve the rope after descending.

Belayed Climbing
When removing large trees with extensive lower branching, it may be advantageous to pre-install the climbing line in the tree to facilitate moving past the limbs. If the climber is using a micro pulley as a slack tender, a ground person can provide a belay by "tailing" the rope or holding down on the running end of the climbing line. This enables the pulley to advance the friction hitch and free the climber's hands to climb the tree and advance the lanyard.

Tricks of the Trade: Adjustable False Crotch (AFC)

The adjustable false crotch is an advanced technique which offers climbers an excellent backup when removing hazardous trees whose structural integrity is questionable. The AFC is installed in a neighboring tree and therefore provides an outstanding escape route if a hazard such as bees is encountered, or if the tree actually begins to fail while the climber is in it. This system also provides the climber with a second point of balance, which is particularly useful when climbing trees having an extreme lean or when working the underside of the tree. An additional benefit the AFC offers is the ability for a ground person to effectively lower the climber in the event of an emergency. The AFC can be integrated with any of the entry and lowering methods requiring a rope.

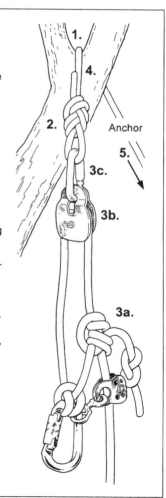

Setting up the Adjustable False Crotch

1 Install an anchor line over a secure crotch in a nearby tree (1). This tree should be the tallest and closest to the one being removed. The higher the line is installed the more effective the system will be.

2 Tie a Figure Eight on a Bight in one end of the anchor line (2).

3 Rig a traditional or split-tail climbing system (3a) through an approved pulley (3b). Attach the system to the Figure Eight knot with a double-locking carabiner (3c).

4 Raise the false crotch until the Figure Eight knot is at a point just below the natural crotch (4). Be sure to hold or anchor the working end of the climbing system before raising it.

5 Secure the anchor line to the base of the tree using a figure-8 descender tied off using the "hard lock" method (p. 66). In the event of an emergency, the ground person has the option of lowering the climber to the ground without having to climb the tree.

6 Clip-in to the climbing system and take up rope slack while climbing or a ground person can "tail" the rope through a micro pulley instead.

7 If the climber must "bail out" or escape from the tree, his or her lanyard must first be released before swinging into the neighboring tree.

Warning! To avoid a potentially long and uncontrolled swing the AFC must be anchored high and as close to the tree being climbed as possible. A ground person can also slow the swing by providing a belay on the running end of the climbing line.

P—Positioning in the Tree

After entering the tree, the climber's goal is to attain a position that allows him or her to work aloft safely and comfortably. Good positioning technique will also provide the means for accessing the outer branches of the tree. In addition, the climber must be aware of his or her position, in relation to the ground, when planning and performing a descent.

The techniques described in this section of the book enable the climber to: 1) tie in to the tree and climbing line with a suitable climbing system, 2) advance and recrotch the climbing line, 3) fine tune the climber's position in situations and locations in the tree that are awkward and difficult to access, and 4) prepare for and execute a safe and efficient descent from the tree. The positioning steps and techniques include:

1. Tying in
2. Rope Advance
3. Limb Walking
4. Recrotching
5. Double Crotching
6. Redirects
7. Descending

It is absolutely necessary that the climber has two means of tying in to the tree while climbing and working aloft. Whenever the climber unclips from the climbing system to advance or recrotch the climbing line he or she must be secured by one means and be secured by both when operating a chain saw. In addition, the climber must not climb above the original tie-in point without first tying in with a second lanyard or line to prevent a potential fall and swing.

The Weak Link Law Revisited

We began our examination of the P.R.E.P. system on page 10 with the weak link illustration, and discussing about how it related to the implementation of each step of the system. Now is a good time to revisit this principle as a prelude to the discussion of "tying in" on the following pages.

It is vital that the climber understand how each component in the climbing system is like the link in a chain. If one link fails the entire chain fails. Each component, therefore, requires the climber's careful inspection, installation, and operation. As more components, or links, are added to the system, the climber's burden of responsibility to maintain them increases as well.

Aerial Rescue

Performing an aerial rescue of an injured climber is a rare occurrence. Nevertheless, tree climbers and workers need to prepare for such an event before it occurs. This begins with developing a plan and rescue procedure. For this procedure to be effective, climbers/workers must have proper training, education, and practice with the appropriate equipment. Most accidents can be prevented by observing safe climbing and working practices, many of which are discussed in this book.

---

1. "Tying In"

"Tied in" describes a climber who has properly installed a climbing line using a suitable crotch, branch, or false crotch and has secured the line to the climbing saddle with an approved connecting device, attachment knot (or eye splice), and friction hitch. The term tying in is also used when a climber has secured his or her position with a personal lanyard. The climber needs to tie in as soon as the desired destination in the tree has been reached and each time the climbing line is advanced or recrotched. The procedure for tying in with a climbing line is outlined below.

1. Select a Tie-In Point

The location in the tree where the climber ties in is referred to as the **tie-in point**. The higher the tie-in point the greater the range of mobility the climber will experience when working. The effectiveness of a high tie in can be further enhanced when situated in a position that is central in the tree or, better yet, directly over the work area. Ensure that the selected tie-in point is located so that a slip or fall will swing the climber away from any electrical conductor or other potential hazard.

2. Tie In to the Tree

Once the tie-in point has been selected the climber can tie in to the tree utilizing a **natural crotch** or a **false crotch**.

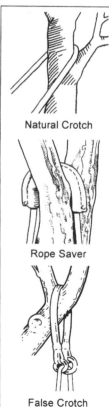

Natural Crotch: To tie in to a natural crotch the climber passes the climbing line around the larger limb or stem of the tree and over the smaller branch. If the smaller branch should break off, the climbing line will slide down the main trunk and catch on the next branch instead of coming out of the tree entirely. It is important to choose a crotch that is wide enough to allow the rope to pass easily, without binding. The leather **rope saver** device (p. 30) can be installed in a natural crotch to protect both the climbing line and tree limb from abrasion. This device truly is a rope saver when placed over the limb of a pitchy conifer tree.

Natural Crotch

Rope Saver

False Crotch: The false crotch device (p. 27) provides an excellent alternative to a natural crotch as a route for the climbing or rigging line. Like the leather rope saver, a false crotch minimizes wear on the climbing line and damage to tree branches by significantly reducing the abrasion that normally occurs at these contact points. The false crotch can also be wrapped around the trunk or stem where no crotch exists.

False Crotch

3. Select a Climbing System

Selecting a climbing system completes the tie in procedure. The two most frequently used systems are the **traditional** and **split-tail** climbing systems. Both are examples of a dynamic climbing line system (p. 35). Beginning climbers should start by learning and becoming proficient with the traditional system before graduating to the "high performance" split-tail system which is more complex and gear intensive.

These systems can be broken down into several components: 1) the climbing line, 2) connecting device (rope snap or carabiner), 3) attachment knot or eye splice (secures the climbing line to the climber's saddle or connecting device), 4) bridge or split tail, 5) friction hitch (secures climber to the running end of the rope), and 6) micro pulley (functions as a slack tender and fair lead). For each component there are a variety of options from which to choose. For a complete selection and description of approved attachment knots and friction hitches turn to page 68. The drawings below show one method of "assembling" the climbing systems using only a few of the many knot and hardware choices available.

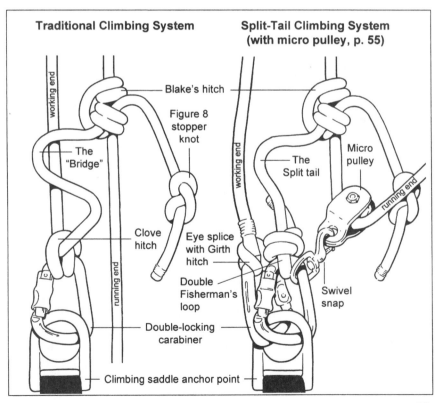

Traditional Climbing System

Split-Tail Climbing System
(with micro pulley, p. 55)

working end

Blake's hitch

Figure 8 stopper knot

The "Bridge"

working end

The Split tail

Micro pulley

running end

Clove hitch

Eye splice with Girth hitch

Double Fisherman's loop

Double-locking carabiner

running end

Swivel snap

Climbing saddle anchor point

A Closer Look at Climbing Systems

The Traditional System

Begin by tying an attachment knot, 3 to 4 feet from the working end of the climbing line to an approved double-locking carabiner or rope snap. "Clip-in" to the center anchor point of the climbing saddle with the connecting device. Tie a friction hitch, with the remaining tail of the climbing line, to the running end. For added safety, tie a Figure Eight stopper knot in the remaining end of the friction hitch.

"Tied in" around a natural crotch with the tradition climbing system.

To eliminate a link in the climbing system, tie the attachment knot directly to the climbing saddle instead of a connecting device. The length of rope between the attachment knot and the friction hitch is called the "bridge." The proper bridge length is determined by the climber's technique, arm length, and personal preference.

The Split-tail System

This system is constructed by securing the working end of the climbing line to a suitable connecting device with either an approved attachment knot or eye spliced end. With this system the rope end is terminated without leaving a tail. Instead, a separate length of rope or **split tail** is used to form the bridge from the climber's saddle to the running end of the rope where it is tied off with a suitable friction hitch. Both the working end of the climbing line and the end of the split tail are connected to the central anchor point of the climbing saddle, or when provided, separate anchor points. This arrangement allows the climber to recrotch or, when using the climbing line as a second lanyard, pass limbs without having to untie and retie the friction hitch. Instead the climber simply unclips the working end of the climbing line (after securing his or her position with a safety lanyard), repositions the line, and then clips back in.

Split tails range in length from four to six feet long (before the knots are tied) and must meet industry standards for climbing lines. Many climbers use a different colored line for the split tail for easy recognition. As split tails become worn they can be discarded and replaced without having to cut off tail sections from the primary line. Both the traditional and split-tail climbing systems can be further enhanced by attaching a **micro pulley** to the climbing line below the friction hitch to function as a "fair lead" and slack tender.

Tools of the Trade: Micro Pulley

The micro pulley is a small and inexpensive tool that performs a variety of useful tasks. It is most commonly used as a means for tending slack in the climbing line and adjusting the length of a personal lanyard. When used for this purpose the micro pulley is appropriately referred to as a "slack tender." The pulley is attached to the climbing line or lanyard just below (or behind) the friction hitch. It is secured with a carabiner or swivel snap (dog leash snap) to the climber's saddle or the primary connecting device (Fig. a, b).

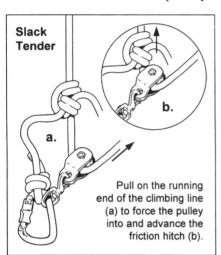

Slack Tender

a.

b.

Pull on the running end of the climbing line (a) to force the pulley into and advance the friction hitch (b).

As the climber pulls on the running end of the rope (Fig. a) the micro pulley is forced into and advances the friction hitch on the climbing line or lanyard (Fig. b). This feature allows the climber to manage rope slack with only one hand. For this reason the micro pulley serves the climber well during limb walk returns.

The micro pulley can also be operated or "tailed" by a ground worker. This method provides an effective belay when the climber is tied in with a dynamic climbing system and entering the tree with a ladder, the body thrust technique, or climbing spurs. The belayer simply holds the running end of the climbing line taut and the micro pulley advances the friction hitch for the climber.

Another use of the micro pulley is to maintain a direct line or **fair lead** from the climbing line to the friction hitch. This is most evident when the running end of the line is over a branch above or away from the climber and causes the rope to bind preventing the friction hitch to slide properly. The micro pulley redirects the rope into the friction hitch so it can be operated effectively. A carabiner can be substituted for the micro pulley with reasonable success.

"Fair Lead"

The micro pulley "fair leads" the climbing line and allows one-handed slack control.

2. Rope Advance

Advancing the climbing line to a position higher in the tree can radically increase the climber's range of mobility. In most instances, this will be the first thing the climber will do after reaching the canopy. The benefits of a high tie-in point cannot be overemphasized. The advantages become evident when moving out on long lateral limbs. The best techniques for advancing the climbing line include the alternate lanyard technique, throwline, throwing knot, and pole saw and pruner. These techniques may have to be repeated several times during the climb before the "target" crotch or tie in is reached. The climber must be secured at all times when performing them.

Using the throwline to advance the climbing line.

Alternate Lanyard Technique (ALT): When the tree's branch spacing is relatively close, the climber may advance his or her position and climbing line by using the ALT. For many climbers this technique is the first choice in gaining access to the highest locations in the tree.

Throwline: The throwline is a versatile tool to use while working aloft to advance the climbing line, set up a double crotch, or set a line in a neighboring tree that may be climbed next. In addition, the throwline can be lowered to a ground worker and used to send up tools or a dropped rope. A small line bag can be attached to the climbing saddle with a carabiner and used to store the throwline and throwbag while aloft (nylon line stuffs better than polyethylene line).

Throwing Knot: For short throws within the canopy the throwing knot is hard to beat as a means of advancing the climbing line. The knot can be tied so it stays locked for repeated throws, or for the easy shots, unlocked, so it will unwind after the shot is made. Keep in mind that a stuck throwing knot could potentially trap the climber in position.

Pole Saw/Pruner: The extension of reach that the pole saw and pruner provide make it a practical tool enabling the climber to set and advance the climbing line, prune branches, or grab hangers. It is an excellent means of advancing the line when the climber is directly below the "target" crotch making throwing a difficult option. A version of the throwing knot is set on the backside of the saw or pruner, away from the cutting edge, and placed in the crotch. Hang the pole saw so the blade is on the opposite side of the limb from the climber.

3. Limb Walking

Limb walking is an essential skill to learn for work positioning in the tree. This skill enables climbers to walk out to the ends of tree limbs using the climbing line as another point of balance. The most proficient limb walkers move about gracefully and freely within the tree, appearing as though they "belong up there." They rely heavily on their climbing line in addition to their developed sense of balance and technique. The use of a personal lanyard coupled with limb walking skills will oftentimes be sufficient for providing climbers with a good work position in the tree.

It is important to maintain constant tension on the climbing line while limb walking.

The preferred method of walking out on limbs is to walk sideways or backwards, while maintaining tension on the climbing line. It is generally considered easier to "go out on a limb" than it is to return from limb walking. Going out usually requires only one hand operation to control the friction hitch, freeing the other hand for balancing and performing tasks such as making pruning cuts or installing a redirect (p. 60) or personal lanyard. Pay attention to the angle of the climbing line while walking out on limbs away from the tie-in point. As the climbing line angle increases so does the risk of the climber taking a long and uncontrolled swing in the event of a fall. To minimize this risk tie in with a personal lanyard or redirect as soon as possible.

Returning from limb walks is a more awkward task to perform. Proper rope tension must be maintained by using one hand to pull and hold on the running end of the line, while the other hand advances the friction hitch. This situation can be remedied with the use of a micro pulley. This device not only allows the climber to tend rope slack with one hand but "fair leads" the climbing line into the friction hitch as well.

There are many limb walking techniques that will only be learned and discovered through experimentation. Many movement techniques used in rock climbing are applicable to tree climbing. These include using the hands and feet to jam in crotches or wrap under and around limbs for balance. An artificial foot hold can be produced by Girth hitching a webbing sling or Prusik loop around a suitable limb (p. 63).

4. Recrotching

Another technique which improves the climber's work position is recrotching the climbing line to a new location in the tree. The same techniques used to advance the climbing line are effective for recrotching as well. Unlike the previous technique of advancing the rope to a position higher in the tree, recrotching is simply repositioning the climbing line in a different location—sometimes even lower in the canopy than the original tie in.

Even though the rope advance techniques work well for recrotching by providing the climber with an extension of reach, it is perhaps just as common that the climber will simply climb up or out to the new tie in location to recrotch. While still secured to one end of the climbing line, the climber recrotches by pulling up the opposite end and places it in the new tie-in point using a natural or false crotch. Using the opposite end of the climbing line for recrotching is also referred to as **double rope end climbing**. The climber must add a second means of securing his or her position to perform this operation if the angle of the primary tie in is too great or when it is desirable to recrotch using the same end of the line as the original tie in.

The rope from the original tie in can then be retrieved by unclipping the working end of the climbing line, removing the connecting device, and pulling it back to the climbers new position. The carabiner or rope snap is removed to prevent jamming during retrieval or hitting the climber in the head or face. When using a false crotch or rope saver with the tie in, remember to tie a stopper knot in the rope end for retrieval.

Communication—Command and Response System

Many accidents that occur in the field result from poor communication between workers, primarily between climbers and the ground crew. Therefore, it is essential that an effective command and response system be developed and employed. When a worker initiates a command, he or she does not proceed until an audible response has been given and heard. Visual signals can also be an effective way of communicating, such as giving a "thumbs up" sign. When things really get noisy, a plastic whistle is hard to beat and at times, can be a life saver. Below are a few samples of how an audible command and response system can be used.

Command	Response	Sample Application
Stand clear	(All) Clear	A climber's warning before cutting a limb.
Headache!	(act fast)	An urgent warning, something is heading groundward.
Slack	OK	Release rope tension caused from ground debris.
Up rope	Rope up	Alerting the climber when returning a rigging line.
Going under	OK	A worker about to enter the climber's drop zone.

5. Double Crotching

Double crotching is a positioning technique used when the climber needs an added measure of safety and stability. It is often employed during long limb walks. Double crotching incorporates the use of a second tie-in point installed in the same tree as the primary tie or in another tree. The second tie-in point is attained in the same manner as when recrotching, by installing the opposite end of the rope or a separate climbing line in a crotch using one of the rope advance techniques. In most instances, all that is required to accomplish this is to simply "lob" a throwing knot (or throwbag) over a nearby overhead branch. When tied in the open form, the knot will conveniently unwind back down to the climber for tying in.

Climbers will benefit greatly from the double crotch technique when limb walking on weak or slippery limbs (from ice, snow, or rain). If the second crotch selected is located overhead and directly vertical to the climber's position, almost all the climber's weight may be transferred from the primary tie in to the second. This situation will enable the climber to literally "hover" over the work area without placing any weight on the limb below. This is highly effective when working over obstructions such as antennas, satellite dishes, and electrical conductors. Double crotching is also useful during cabling and bracing operations and when traversing from one tree to another.

The climber needs to be aware that the remaining loop of rope may not be long enough to allow the climber to safely reach the ground or for ground workers to send up tools. The climber may use an attached throwbag and line for the latter purpose. Usually the climber will transfer back over to a single crotch system before descending to ensure enough rope is available for a safe landing. The climber should be secured before untying and retrieving the unwanted climbing system to prevent an unexpected swing. Remove the connecting device before clearing the line!

Double crotching is especially effective when limb walking and working over obstructions.

6. Redirects

There are two techniques for redirecting the climbing line (or rigging line) while working in the tree—the **mechanical redirect** and **natural redirect**. Both techniques fine-tune the climber's position in the tree by providing an improved working angle without having to recrotch the climbing line. Redirects also reduce the chance of an uncontrolled swing as a climber performs a limb walk and works further away from the original tie-in point.

Mechanical Redirects

A mechanical redirect consists of either a rope loop or webbing sling attached to a pear-shaped, double-locking carabiner (both the sling and carabiner must meet industry strength standards). The redirect is rigged by choking the sling to a sturdy branch with a Girth hitch or Basket hitch and placing both strands of the climbing line through the carabiner. The climbing line then assumes a new angle originating from the redirect. A redirect positioned above the climber's position will provide the best work angle. The climber must keep in mind, while descending or moving away from this more effective position, that the redirect must be retrieved by returning to that location.

An advanced technique (not pictured) which enables the climber to retrieve the redirect while in another location in the tree or from the ground involves the use of a false crotch device as the redirect. In this case the false crotch device must be fitted with rings that open such as a carabiner or screw link. The redirect is Basket hitched over a suitable limb while each leg of the doubled climbing line is clipped into its own separate ring. The redirect is retrieved by tying a stopper knot in the end of the rope and pulling down on the other end. The knot will first pass through the large ring of the redirect, around the natural crotch, and back to the redirect where it catches on the small ring, allowing it to be pulled back to the climber.

A redirect provides an improved angle to work from without having to recrotch the climbing line.

Natural Redirects

A natural redirect is when the climbing line is redirected using a natural crotch in the tree. To utilize a natural redirect, the climber drops down through a suitable crotch found along the branch. It is important to avoid using tight crotches which could bind the rope or jam the friction hitch during a rope retrieval later on. As the climber moves onto the limb below, the climbing line is redirected from the crotch above providing a better position to perform work by allowing access to the outer limbs.

If the climber desires to return to the original position on the branch above, it is recommended that he or she use the modified body thrust technique. However, because of the increased friction of the natural redirect, returning can sometimes be a difficult and fatiguing process.

By not clearing the tail of the running end of the climbing line through the redirect, the climber can regain the use of the original tie in without climbing back up. This technique (shown at right) can be applied anytime while working the tree when it is necessary to regain the original point of tie in. Having a pole saw or pruner handy is a good insurance policy in case the knot becomes jammed in the crotch during retrieval.

Use open, U-shaped crotches for natural redirects.

Repositioning the Climbing Line

1 Secure your position in the tree with a personal lanyard.

2 Unclip from the climbing line and tighten the friction hitch so it doesn't slide, or attach the carabiner to a Clove hitch tied just above the friction hitch.

3 Disconnect the micro pulley (if using one).

4 If using the split-tail system, join the running end of the line to the end of the split tail (the traditional climbing system is less likely to jam).

5 Pull down on the running end of the climbing line to clear the rope from the redirect and clip back in.

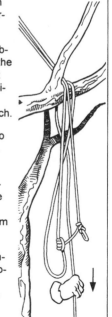

Tools of the Trade: Webbing Slings

Webbing slings (endless loops) and runners (webbing with loops on two ends) have been for many years the ultimate workhorse for rock climbers, cavers, and emergency rescue workers. Tree climbers have also discovered their value as a tool that is inexpensive, strong, and perhaps above all, incredibly versatile. In addition, they are lightweight and compact, enabling users to stuff them into tool pouches or wrap them into a "daisy chain" (p. 92) to be clipped onto the climber's saddle with a carabiner.

Webbing Strength

The webbing slings most commonly used by the professional tree climber are constructed from tubular webbing. Although it appears flat, tubular webbing actually is hollow. One inch wide tubular webbing has a breaking strength of 4,000 pounds. When doubled, to fashion a sling, the breaking strength increases to 8,000 pounds. Deduct the strength loss from joining the ends, (Using the Beer knot, for instance, results in a 20% strength loss.) and you still end up with a sling with a breaking strength exceeding 6,400 pounds. A factory sewn sling will be stronger yet. This exceeds industry requirements for climbing lines (and webbing slings when used as a part of a fall protection system) which is a minimum breaking strength of 5,400 pounds.

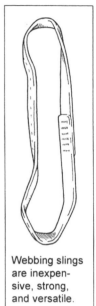

Webbing slings are inexpensive, strong, and versatile.

If more strength is required to safely perform the task, the sling can be doubled using the Basket hitch. By doing so, the sling strength is doubled, depending on such factors as anchor diameter, the angle between the "legs" of the sling as they approach the carabiner, and where the knot is placed in the rigging configuration. The Girth hitch, on the other hand, will downgrade the rated strength of a sling by 25 percent. Nevertheless, the Girth hitch is extremely useful and still provides more than enough strength in most common tree climbing applications.

Making Webbing Slings

Webbing slings are inexpensive whether you make your own or buy the factory sewn variety. To make a webbing sling, begin with purchasing the material from a reputable dealer. Many climbers use different colored webbing to code the slings for function or length. Next, determine the sling's length, allowing about 22 inches for the Water knot and 15 inches for the Beer knot, and cut and heat seal the ends. Finally, join the ends with the traditional, easy-to-tie Water knot or the more difficult, but stronger and neater Beer knot. Sewn slings are also popular options and although slightly more costly, are considered the neatest (no tails or knots to snag on things) and strongest.

The Versatile Webbing Sling

1 Redirect. Redirecting the climbing line is often vital for providing the climber with a more comfortable and safer work position in the tree. Redirect slings reserved specifically for rigging are equally effective when used in conjunction with blocks and lowering lines in directing the load away from obstacles below.

2 Speedline Sling. Webbing slings are the primary vehicle for securing limbs to be cut and sent down a speedline to a ground worker below.

3 False Crotch. A webbing sling can be fashioned into a false crotch for a climbing line by attaching a double-locking pearabiner to one end of the sling and a small screw link to the other end (see pp. 28-29 to install and retrieve).

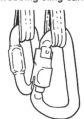

4 Choker. Slide a long sling, or several slings Girth hitched together, under a pile of brush and choker the pile together. Use the remaining loop as a handle for dragging by hand or machine.

5 Foot loop. A webbing sling, when secured to the trunk or a limb, can provide the climber with a temporary foothold, thereby providing a better position to work from. They

can also be attached to handled ascenders as a footloop when using the SRT.

6 Tool Lanyard. Webbing slings make excellent lanyards for chainsaws and cabling tools or as a means to attach anything that needs to be stored in the tree or sent up the tree to the climber. When used as a chainsaw lanyard, it should be designed to "break away" in the event it is pulled from the climber's grasp.

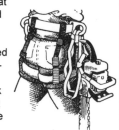

7 Personal Lanyard. A sling becomes a backup to the primary lanyard when Girth hitched around a stem or limb and secured to the climbing saddle. This arrangement also allows climbers to hang on the sling and rest, taking the load off their feet when using climbing spurs.

8 Anchor. Webbing slings can be used to attach a pulley, block or come-along during cabling (below) and rigging operations.

When attached to one or two carabiners, a sling can be used in lieu of a pulley when lowering small branches. A sling can also function as a "third hand" when removing a limb that is too small to lower. Girth hitch one end of the sling around the limb to be removed and hold the other end with one hand, or secure it to the tree until the cut is made. Afterwards, remove the sling and toss the limb.

9 Rope Grab. Webbing slings make reasonably good rope grabs during rigging operations when secured to the rope using either the Klemheist knot or French Prusik. It will be necessary to take more wraps with the sling than is required when using Prusik cord.

7. Descending

The final positioning consideration for the tree climber is planning the descent from the tree after work is completed. There are several descending techniques from which to choose, depending on the climbing system being used.

Descending on a Dynamic Climbing Line System

The climber's first concern, when tied in to a dynamic climbing line system, is to determine if there is enough rope to reach the ground. This can be determined by pulling up and holding the running or free end of the climbing line and looking down to see if the loop formed from the doubled line touches the ground. If it does, there is enough rope to descend. If not, the climber must recrotch to a position lower in the tree before descending.

Secondly, the climber must consider his or her position in the tree in relation to the ground. Will a direct vertical descent subject the climber to any hazards or obstacles located in the tree or on the ground—electrical hazards, structures, areas of water or mud? If so, the climber may need to recrotch or reposition the climbing line to avoid them.

To descend, the climber grasps the friction hitch with one hand and the climbing line below the hitch with the other (held near the hip to help control descent speed) and gently slides the hitch downward. The descent should be slow and controlled to avoid heat damage to the climbing line from excessive friction. A good safety precaution is to tie a Figure Eight stopper knot (p. 71) on the end of the climbing line. This knot prevents the line from accidentally pulling through the friction hitch. After reaching the ground, remove the connecting device and announce an audible "stand clear!" before clearing the line.

Descending on a Static Climbing Line System

One technique that is commonly used to descend either a single or doubled climbing line is to use a figure-8 descender (p. 66). A backup or belay is necessary to secure the climber from an uncontrolled descent or when it becomes necessary to perform limited work along the way down. If managed properly, a Prusik loop tied to the line above the figure-8 provides one means of backing up the descent system. The Prusik loop requires careful attention to how it is tied and operated if it is to function properly. A safer method of backup is with a ground belay. This is performed by the ground person who simply holds or pulls down on the running end of the line. This action creates added friction to the figure-8 allowing the belayer to control the climber's descent from below.

Another descending option, which is limited to a single rope descent, is to use the *Petzel Stop* descending device or other manufacturers' equivalent. Like the figure-8, friction and descent speed is managed with the control hand (hand on running end of line and hip) not the device itself. This tool is self braking as well, stopping the climber's descent as soon as the handle is released.

The Figure-8 Descent
(with Prusik Loop Backup)

This method of descent can be performed on a single line when using the SRT or on a double line when using the secured footlock technique.

1 Attach the figure-8 to the climbing line by following the procedure on page 66. Attach the figure-8 to the climbing saddle with a suitable connecting device. (The climber must be secured while performing this operation.)

2 Tie the Prusik loop to the climbing line above the figure-8 using either a Prusik or Klemheist knot. Ensure that the hitch grips properly when weight is applied. Extra wraps may have to be added. Attach the Prusik loop to the central anchor point on the saddle with a separate connecting device.

3 Slide the friction hitch gently downward, releasing the belay, and use the control hand (the one gripping the rope below the figure-8) to manage the descent speed.

Stop at any point during the descent by squeezing the rope with the control hand held tightly against the hips. To activate the self belay, slowly lower your weight onto the friction hitch until it grips properly.

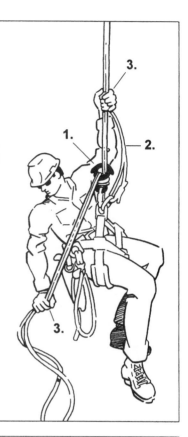

The *Petzel Stop*

The *Stop* is designed for single rope use only on lines up to 1/2 inch in diameter. The rope is threaded around fixed pulley wheels (capstans) inside an aluminum frame. Installation instructions are stamped on the outside of the frame.

The handle on the back of the device acts like an "ON-OFF" switch. When squeezed, the climber descends. When released the cam brake is activated, stopping the climber.

Descent speed is managed with the control hand (hand on running end of line) not with the device itself. Unlike the figure-8, the *Stop* can be rigged without removing it from the saddle.

Tools of the Trade: Figure-8 Device

The figure-8 is a friction device that tree workers employ in a variety of ways. It can be used to descend on a single line (SRT) or doubled line when using the secured footlock method. When anchored to the base of the tree with an anchor sling, using a Timber hitch or Cow hitch, the figure-8 functions as a means for belaying a climber, anchoring a climbing system (SRT and AFC), and lowering limbs or climbers safely to the ground. A variety of styles are available, but the "rescue-8" in either steel construction (used for rigging) or in aluminum, is perhaps the most versatile and preferred by tree workers. Use the illustrations and description below to install and "lock-off" a rope with the figure-8.

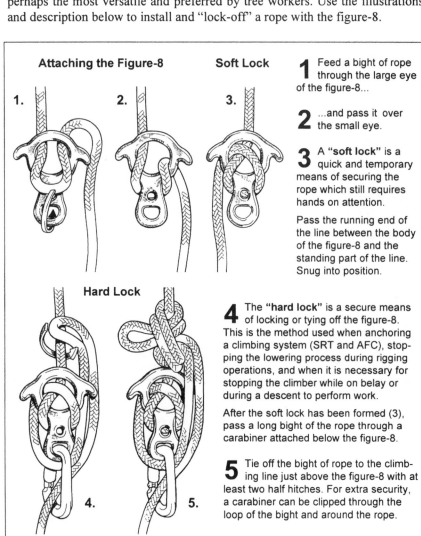

Attaching the Figure-8

1.

2.

Soft Lock

3.

Hard Lock

4.

5.

1 Feed a bight of rope through the large eye of the figure-8...

2 ...and pass it over the small eye.

3 A "soft lock" is a quick and temporary means of securing the rope which still requires hands on attention.

Pass the running end of the line between the body of the figure-8 and the standing part of the line. Snug into position.

4 The "hard lock" is a secure means of locking or tying off the figure-8. This is the method used when anchoring a climbing system (SRT and AFC), stopping the lowering process during rigging operations, and when it is necessary for stopping the climber while on belay or during a descent to perform work.

After the soft lock has been formed (3), pass a long bight of the rope through a carabiner attached below the figure-8.

5 Tie off the bight of rope to the climbing line just above the figure-8 with at least two half hitches. For extra security, a carabiner can be clipped through the loop of the bight and around the rope.

Knots for Tree Climbers

Almost every aspect of tree climbing and tree work involves the use of a rope. In order to employ the rope it is necessary to use knots. Therefore, it is vital that tree climbers and ground workers develop the ability to tie knots correctly, confidently and at times, quickly. In addition, it is essential that climbers select knots that are appropriate to the situation.

On the pages that follow are over twenty five different knots commonly used by tree climbers and ground workers. Knowing only a handful of the "core" knots (Bowline, Clove hitch, Cow/Girth hitch, Blake's hitch, and Munter hitch) will enable the climber to effectively climb and perform work in the tree. At

> "A knot is never nearly right; it is either exactly right or it is hopelessly wrong, one or the other; there is nothing in between."
>
> *Clifford Ashley*

some point, however, it will be necessary for climbers to learn more knots to increase their level of climbing and working proficiency. Fortunately, many of the core knots provide the foundation for learning other knots as well, facilitating the process.

Brion Toss, a well known rigger, writer, and knot expert, suggests carrying around a six-foot hank of one-eighth to one-quarter inch diameter rope. It's small enough to fit unnoticed in a pocket and is always available to practice knots at odd moments (waiting in line or traffic delays, lunch breaks, etc.). In addition, the rope will frequently be useful in everyday practical situations.

Tie, Dress, and Set (TDS)

Tying knots involves more than just making the "rabbit come out of the hole, go around the tree, and back in the hole" as with the Bowline. A properly tied knot must also be **finished** properly by **dressing** and **setting** it. Dressing the knot means properly aligning, arranging, or straightening all the parts of the knot so it matches the description and picture in the book. Knot and rope strength can be significantly reduced if the knot is dressed improperly.

Setting the knot involves tightening all its parts so they properly touch, grab, and press against each other. This creates friction on the rope—the reason a knot works. A knot that is loosely tied could "capsize" and come untied when a load is applied. It is good practice to periodically inspect knots while in use to ensure they remain tied. New knots should never be employed aloft until they can be skillfully tied, dressed, and set (**TDS**) while on the ground.

Knot Characteristics

A good knot is easy to tie, inspect, and untie after loading. In addition, climbers will often select knots that are compact in size (compare the Buntline hitch with the Figure Eight knot) and/or are versatile in their application (Bowline and Clove hitch). Finally, a good knot provides the strength and security necessary to safely perform the intended tasks.

Knot Categories, Selection, and Application

Attachment Knots have multi-purpose application for fastening or anchoring a line to something. They are used as **end-line** or **tie-in** knots to attach the end of the climbing line or lanyard to the climber's saddle or, more commonly, a carabiner or rope snap. Some can be used to attach a throwline to a throwbag or climbing line. Attachment knots are commonly used during rigging operations to secure limbs for lowering, anchor slings to a tree, or to send items to the climber working aloft.

Attachment Knots	Page	Application	
		Tying In	Rigging/ Attach.
Bowline	70	✓	✓
Figure Eight	71	✓	✓
Buntline Hitch	72	✓	
Anchor Hitch	73	✓	✓
Double Fisher-man's Loop	74	✓	
Clove Hitch	75	✓	✓
Running Bowline	76		✓
Cow and Girth Hitch	77		✓
Basket Hitch	77		✓
Timber Hitch	78		✓
Sheet Bend	79		✓
Quick Hitch	80		✓
Pile Hitch	22		✓

Friction Hitches are sometimes referred to as "climbing knots", when they function as a "rope grab" device to self belay the climber while ascending or descending on either a dynamic or static climbing line system. They are often used as a mid-line attachment point during rigging operations also. Friction hitches secure the climber or load by grabbing the rope when under tension. When the tension is eased the hitch can be disabled and moved up or down the rope.

The Munter hitch, although classified as a friction hitch, performs in a different way than as a rope grab. This versatile hitch provides sufficient friction for belaying a climber, lowering small limbs, and descending on a static climbing line.

Friction Hitches	Page	Application	
		Split Tail	Traditional System
Munter Hitch	81	(belay & descend)	
Tautline Hitch	82	✓	✓
Blake's Hitch	83	✓	✓
French Prusik	84	✓	
Prusik Knot	86	✓	✓
Klemheist	87	✓	

Mid-Line Knots are used primarily during rigging operations when a mid-rope anchor point is needed for quick carabiner clip-ins.

Mid-Line Knots	Page	Application
Butterfly Knot	88	light rigging
Bowline on a Bight	89	heavy rigging

Bends (End-to-End Tie-Offs) are tied in rope to form Prusik loops or in webbing to form slings/endless loops.

Bends	Page	Material Tied in	
		Rope	Webbing
Double Fisherman's	90	✓	
Sliding Double Fisherman's	91	✓	
Water Knot	92		✓
Beer Knot	93		✓

Knot Terminology

bend: A knot that joins two rope, cord, or webbing ends together.

bight: A doubled section of rope that does not cross itself.

hitch: A knot that secures a rope to an object or the rope's own standing part.

knot: A general term referring to all knots, hitches, and bends.

loop: A turn or bight that crosses itself.

running end: The end of the rope not being used to tie or rig with.

standing part: The inactive part of the rope uninvolved with rigging or knots.

round turn: Two *turns* of rope around an object.

turn: One round of rope passing around an object.

working end: The end of the rope used to rig or tie off to something.

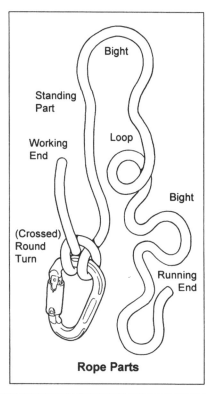

Rope Parts

Coiling Rope—The Gasket Hitch Method

Rope bags, buckets, and tarps work fine for storing ropes, but there is no better way to dry out wet ropes than to coil them and hang them up to dry—and it takes a knot to do that too. The Gasket hitch is a good knot for coiling rope to be stored and/or dried. It also is commonly used to form a quick throwing knot.

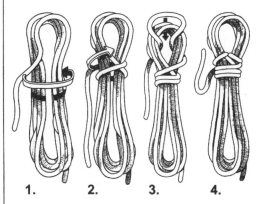

1.   **2.**   **3.**   **4.**

1 Coil up all but the last 4 to 5 feet of rope.

2 Make several horizontal turns around the coils.

3 Push a bight of the end through the space above the turns. Open the bight, sliding over the coils...

4 ...down to the top of the turns. Pull the end to set. Hang from the top loops or a knot tied in the end of the tail.

Bowline

The Bowline is considered one of the "core" knots that all tree climbers and workers should master. It is used primarily as a "tie-in" or end-line knot, to attach the climbing line to a rope snap or carabiner. It is also used for attaching a throwline to a throwbag. The Bowline provides the foundation for tying the Running Bowline and Bowline on a Bight. It is a strong knot that's easy to tie, inspect, and untie, even after heavy loading.

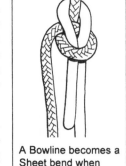

A Bowline becomes a Sheet bend when tied in separate lines.

The Bowline does have a tendency to creep and potentially work loose, particularly in stiffer and slicker climbing lines. Therefore, it is strongly recommended that the Bowline be made more secure by using the **Yosemite Tie-Off**, especially when used as a rope termination with the split-tail climbing system. This tie-off also orients the tail in a better position to tie a friction hitch to the running end of the line when using the traditional climbing system.

Single Bowline

Bowline with Yosemite Tie-Off

1 Form a loop in the standing part of the rope and insert the end into it from below. Pass the end around the standing part and back into the loop.

2 After tying a single Bowline use the remaining tail to follow the path of the originally formed loop up through the eye and parallel to the standing part.

3 Set the knot by holding the standing part and the tail with one hand and with the other hand pull and work the bottom loop until properly tightened.

The remaining tail can be tied off to the standing part with an Overhand or Double-fisherman's knot or be used as the "bridge" for tying the friction hitch.

Caution! When tying the Single Bowline be sure the tail ends up on the inside of the major loop instead of the outside. The knot's strength is not reduced if tied backwards but it is more vulnerable to snagging and potentially capsizing the knot, resulting in a Slip knot.

Figure Eight on a Bight

The preferred attachment knot of most rock climbers, cavers, and high angle rope technicians for tying in to the end of the climbing line is the Figure Eight on a Bight (bottom). It is a versatile knot that is easy to tie and inspect. It provides a quick and secure loop that can be formed mid-rope if necessary, a feature that allows for quick clip-ins with carabiners when using either the split-tail or traditional climbing system. Like the Bowline, the tail of the Figure Eight is properly aligned to function as the "bridge" for the friction hitch.

The disadvantages of the Figure 8 knot are that it's bulky, taking about twice the rope to tie than other attachment knots, and is somewhat difficult to untie after being only moderately loaded.

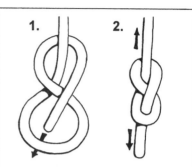

The Figure Eight stopper knot is tied at the end of a rope to prevent it from slipping through the friction hitch when descending or a pulley when returning the rope to the climber. It is often tied in the tail of a knot, such as the Tautline hitch, to make it more secure.

The Figure Eight knot can also be used to secure the throwline to the throwbag (p. 22).

Figure Eight on a Bight

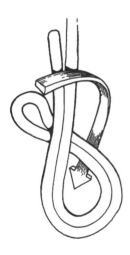

1 Form a bight in the rope, pass the end behind the standing part, then in front of the standing part...

2 ...and down through the loop. Keep both parts of the line parallel, and set the knot by pulling the opposite ends.

3 The loop in the knot needs only to be big enough to contain the carabiner clipped into it (applies to Bowline also).

Buntline Hitch

Nautical books are filled with praise of the Buntline hitch as an extremely simple, quick tying, compact, and secure hitch. This is a lesser known hitch with the professional tree climber, but those who have discovered it like it with good reason. The same virtues that have attracted seaman to the Buntline also hold true for the tree climber. The Buntline functions as an end-line knot for attaching the climbing line or personal lanyard to a connecting device, such as a rope snap or carabiner. Closer inspection of the Buntline will reveal that it is simply a Clove hitch tied around its own standing part. If you learn to tie the Clove hitch first, the Buntline will be easy to learn.

Of all the end-line attachment knots, the Buntline requires the least amount of rope length to tie—creating a very compact knot. Perhaps one of its best features, something the Anchor hitch and Double-Fisherman's loop also share, is how the hitch snugs up tightly against the carabiner. This prevents the carabiner from moving around in the knot and allowing the load to shift to the weaker, minor axis. If desired, the Buntline can be finished with a single Overhand or Double Fisherman's knot tied around the standing part for security, although the tail tends not to slip or creep. This hitch is not recommended for rigging because it is inclined to jam under extreme loads. However, even then, it is not difficult to pick apart.

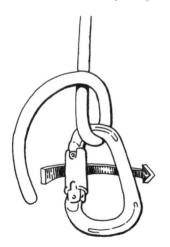 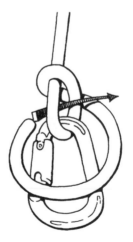 

1 Begin by making a turn around the carabiner, followed with a turn around the standing part.

2 Continue with the end around the turn and make a half hitch around the standing part.

3 Dress, set, and tighten the hitch against the carabiner.

Tools of the Trade: Round and oval rope thimbles are often used with rope snaps and carabiners to reduce wear on the climbing line and minimize strength loss from excessive rope bending.

Anchor Hitch

The knot traditionally used by tree climbers for securing the climbing line to the climber's saddle, rope snap, or carabiner is the Anchor hitch. This is one of the most secure hitches. It is also an excellent choice for attaching the throwline to the throwbag.

The Anchor hitch is slower to tie than the Buntline, especially when tied through the small eye of a rope snap, because the end must go under two turns instead of one. But, like the Buntline hitch, it can be snugged against the carabiner or rope snap, trapping the connecting device in position. In fact, the Anchor hitch probably performs this job better than other hitches because it is wider at the point of attachment providing more surface area of rope to grip the connecting device. When used as an end-line knot for tying in to the split-tail climbing system, the tail can be secured in the same way as the Buntline to make the knot safer, neater, and more secure.

 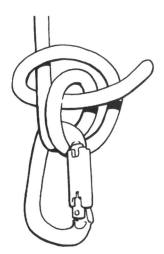 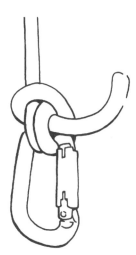

1 Make a complete turn (round turn) around the carabiner or rope snap.

2 Make a half hitch by bringing the rope end around the standing part and through the first turn.

3 Dress, set, and tighten the hitch against the carabiner or rope snap.

How Strong is that Knot?

"Too often, high angle (rope) people worry about knot weaknesses or efficiencies. But it is a proven fact that very few ropes ever break at a knot. Usually an old cut, a worn point, or an abrasion point will cause a rope to fail. Internal weaknesses caused from a fall or grit inside the fibers can also shorten the life of a rope."

From *On Rope* by Bruce Smith and Allen Padgett

Double Fisherman's Loop

The Double Fisherman's Loop (DFL) is simply one half of the Double Fisherman's knot tied around its own standing part. When tied in this fashion the DFL makes an excellent rope termination for lanyards and climbing lines, especially when using the split-tail climbing system. The DFL is difficult to untie after loading and therefore should only be used with carabiners. Unlike rope snaps, carabiners allow the knot to be repositioned toward the gate opening where it can be removed and the knot easily cleared. Some climbers use a triple version of the DFL to acquire even more friction and security.

Like the Buntline and Anchor hitch, the DFL cinches snugly against the carabiner, but instead of the tail exiting the hitch 90 degrees to the standing part it runs neatly along its side. The DFL is also used to form the cord ends when using the Valdâtain tresse and is foundational to learning the Double Fisherman's knot and the Sliding Double Fisherman's knot.

1 Form a bight in the rope and pass the working end around the standing part twice. This may be done with or without the carabiner in place.

2 Tuck the working end through the two loops so that it runs parallel with the standing part.

3 Dress and set the knot tightly against the carabiner. At least three inches of tail should be sticking out.

Eye Splices

Properly made eye splices in the ends of climbing lines, lanyards, and split tails provide a strong, streamlined, and convenient means for attaching rope to rope snaps and carabiners and when installing the climbing line through the closed rings of a false crotch device.

Clove Hitch

Of all the hitches used to secure a line to an object, the Clove hitch is perhaps the best known. It is quick to tie when tied on a bight, provides quick adjustment, and uses a small amount of rope. However, for some applications it is not considered a particularly secure knot, so it must be used with care.

The tree climber will find a variety of uses for this versatile hitch. The Clove hitch can be used to tie off smaller limbs for lowering (when finished with two half hitches), send equipment up to a climber, and attach the throwline to a throwbag or climbing line. When tied on a bight, the Clove hitch provides a quick carabiner attachment for the traditional climbing system. *Do not use the Clove hitch as an end-line knot when using the split-tail climbing system as it could slip and pull the tail through the knot.*

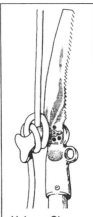

Using a Clove hitch to send a pole saw aloft.

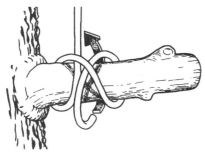

1 Make two crossed round turns and pass the end under the crossed part of the second. Pass the end around...

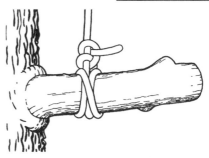

2 ...in the same direction of the established loops and tie two half hitches to the standing part to secure the hitch.

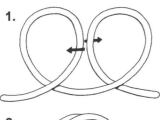

1.

2.

Clove Hitch on a Bight

1 Form two loops in the rope with opposite twists.

2 Pass the right loop in front of the left loop. Draw up tight around object.

The fastest method of tying in to the traditional climbing system is with the Clove hitch tied on a bight (2a). However, this can only be accomplished when using a carabiner.

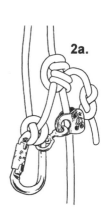

2a.

Running Bowline

The Running Bowline is nothing more than a Bowline tied around its own standing part which allows it to function as a slip knot. This is an outstanding rigging knot that is used to secure tag and lowering lines to limbs, and pull lines to trees during felling operations.

The Running Bowline has a tendency to loosen from the secured object when it is unloaded. Therefore, set the knot tightly and cinch the standing part back on itself at the point of rope contact. Tying a half hitch before the Running Bowline, or Clove hitch when used for the same purpose, can reduce rope deformation by improving the angle by which the rope enters the knot. This procedure is recommended when lowering large and heavy wood. If desired, the Running Bowline may be backed-up with the Yosemite Tie-Off method (p. 70).

The Running Bowline is also useful for anchoring the climbing line when using the single rope technique. The climbing line can be anchored around the base of a tree, or it can be "run up" to the limb the line is crotched over. In the latter application, the knot can be retrieved from the ground by tying the other end of the climbing line or a separate line to the loop of the Bowline. Pulling down on the line will release and return the knot to the climber on the ground. Make certain to climb the running end of the climbing line and not the retrieval line! A common practice of ground workers is to return the working end of the rigging line to a climber aloft by first tying a Running Bowline around the running end of the line. This method allows for a controlled rope return.

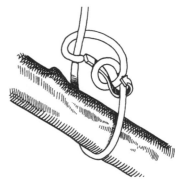

1 Pass the rope around the limb and form a loop in the standing part. Pass the end around the running end and finish like an ordinary Bowline.

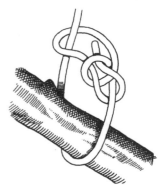

2 Dress and set the knot. Take advantage of any stubs or swellings found along the limb which might help keep the rope from slipping off during the lifting or lowering process and position the loop accordingly.

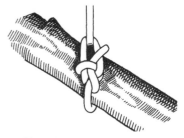

3 Cinch the standing part back on itself at the point of rope contact.

Cow Hitch and Girth Hitch

The Cow hitch and Girth hitch appear identical in knot formation but differ in the material used to tie the hitch. A Cow hitch is tied using a single piece of rope and the Girth hitch is tied using a continuous or endless loop. Both hitches are used interchangeably for securing slings to a tree. When the Cow hitch is used for this purpose the tail must be backed up with a half hitch to make it secure. The Girth hitch is commonly used to secure webbing slings to a limb or trunk as a redirect, foot loop, and anchor point for rigging gear.

Cow Hitch with Anchor Sling

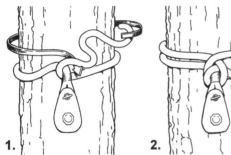

1.   **2.**

1 Pass the working end of the rope around the tree, under the standing part and back around the tree in the opposite direction. Bring the end through the bight formed by the two wraps.

2 Tie a half hitch around the standing part and tuck the tail under one of the wraps leading away from the block. Dress and set.

Girth Hitch with Webbing Sling

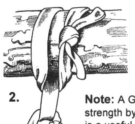

1.   **2.**

1 Pass the sling around the limb or trunk and through itself by passing one end through the other.

2 Dress and set the knot snug against the limb.

Note: A Girth hitch will down grade sling strength by at least 25%. Nevertheless, it is a useful and acceptable hitch that provides more than enough strength for most climbing applications. Use caution when using it in heavy rigging operations.

Basket Hitch

Use the Basket hitch when you need to increase the strength of a sling when used as an anchor. The sling's strength is actually doubled, when configured like the drawing, since the number of "legs" that support the load are also doubled. A sling rated for 8,000 pounds suddenly becomes a 16,000 pound anchor point (minus strength loss from knots or stitching). One of the most common uses of the Basket hitch is to install a false crotch device for a climbing line.

Basket Hitched Sling

Timber Hitch

Like the Cow hitch, the Timber hitch provides a means for securing an anchor sling to the tree trunk for attaching a belay/lowering device, pulleys, and rigging blocks. It is primarily used when attaching the sling around large diameter trunk wood since it takes less rope to tie than does the Cow hitch. This easy to tie hitch is very secure and doesn't jam after it has been loaded making it easy to untie. Unless the hitch is preceded by a half hitch this hitch is not recommended for tying off limbs for lowering because of its potential to "roll out." Even still, the Clove hitch and Running Bowline perform this latter function better.

It is recommended that at least five tucks or turns be made around the standing part for this hitch to function properly. If the sling is too short to take five tucks it will be necessary to use a longer one and perhaps, a heavier one, since the wood the climber is working with is most likely larger and heavier as well. It is important that the sling is loaded vertically (90° to bight) instead of horizontally, which could loosen the hitch.

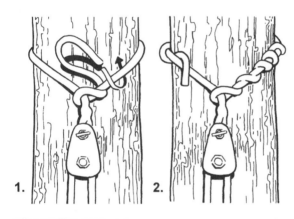

1 Pass the working end of the rope around the tree. Make a turn on the standing part, reversing direction, and make the first tuck back under itself.

2 Continue making a series of tucks that spiral back under itself. Spread the tucks out evenly around the trunk. Five tucks should be considered minimum. Dress and set.

1.

2.

Washing a Rope

Climbing and rigging lines get dirty no matter how well they are cared for and an occasional bath is good for them—when done properly. Begin by doubling the rope and "daisy chaining" it (p. 92) to keep single lines from tangling. Place rope in a netted wash bag or directly into the washing machine (a front loading commercial washer without a central rotating agitator is recommended).

Run the machine through a rinse cycle first if you suspect the previous load contained bleach. Next, set the machine to delicate cycle with cold water. Add a mild soap, such as Ivory Flakes (avoid using a "detergent" which can be harmful to the rope) and run the rope through a wash and rinse cycle. If desired, a non-chlorine fabric softener can be added to the rinse cycle to restore the rope's finish. Finally, undo the chain and let the rope air dry away from direct sunlight.

Sheet Bend

The Sheet bend is one of the few knots that effectively join two ropes of different diameter and type. However, it does not have much application to tree climbing and tree work other than sending a line up to a climber and the Quick hitch is perhaps better suited for this purpose. Nevertheless, many climbers still prefer the Sheet bend and find the Slippery Sheet bend variation just as effective for providing a quick release for separating the joined lines.

When joining ropes of different diameter make sure the smaller line (clear rope in drawing below) is the one tucked under its own standing part. If reversed, the knot is less secure and could slip apart. The Sheet bend is easy to tie and, like the Bowline, easy to untie even after heavy loading. *This hitch is not intended for lengthening climbing lines used for life support or for rigging lines used in potentially life threatening situations.*

Slippery Sheet Bend

1 Form a bight in the climber's (or larger diameter) line. Pass the end of the smaller line (clear) through the open end of the bight and around both standing parts.

2 Finish by passing the end under its own standing part. Pull the standing parts of both ropes to tighten the knot.

Tie the same as the Sheet bend except form a bight in the end and tuck it under the line's own standing part.

Quick Hitch

The origins and actual title of the Quick hitch is uncertain. It appeared in the September 1996 issue of *The Treeworker*, a publication of the National Arborist Association, but with questionable reference to the knot's true identity. Regardless of its uncertain past, it is probably the best knot there is for attaching a rope to a climber's line to be sent aloft. This may be the only use for this knot, but because it is so fast and easy to tie and comes apart effortlessly with a simple yank on the end of the rope, is well worth knowing.

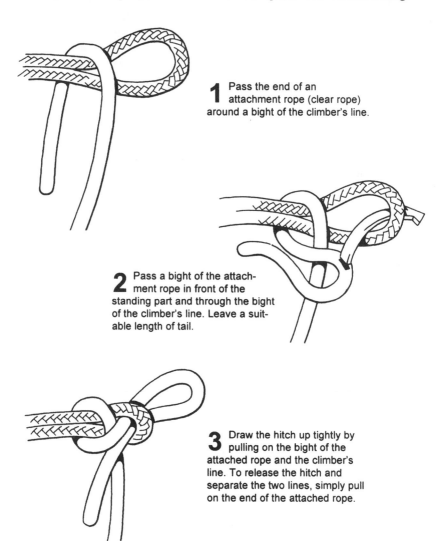

1 Pass the end of an attachment rope (clear rope) around a bight of the climber's line.

2 Pass a bight of the attachment rope in front of the standing part and through the bight of the climber's line. Leave a suitable length of tail.

3 Draw the hitch up tightly by pulling on the bight of the attached rope and the climber's line. To release the hitch and separate the two lines, simply pull on the end of the attached rope.

Munter Hitch

Every tree climber and ground worker should learn the versatile Munter hitch. It is quick and easy to tie and provides an outstanding method for belay while body thrusting or using a ladder to enter the tree. It also allows the climber to lower limbs and descend on the climbing line.

It is important to use only pear-shaped locking carabiners when using the Munter hitch. The wide top of the carabiner will allow this two-

The Munter hitch is useful for belaying a climber or lowering limbs.

directional hitch to invert when switching from raising a load (Fig. 2a) to lowering a load (Fig. 2b) and the locking feature will prevent accidental opening.

The carabiner should be clipped into a suitable anchor sling attached to the tree with either a Cow hitch or Timber hitch. Install it low on the tree to facilitate belay and lowering operation. It is important to keep hands away from the hitch during operation. When used for descending, the Munter hitch must be backed up with a suitable self belay system such as the Prusik loop or split-tail.

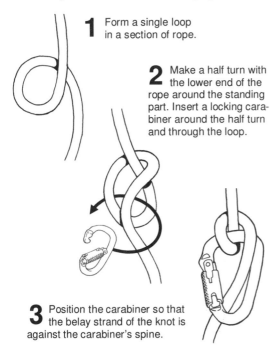

1 Form a single loop in a section of rope.

2 Make a half turn with the lower end of the rope around the standing part. Insert a locking carabiner around the half turn and through the loop.

3 Position the carabiner so that the belay strand of the knot is against the carabiner's spine.

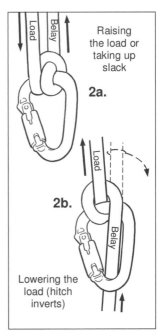

Load | Belay

Raising the load or taking up slack

2a.

Load

2b.

Belay

Lowering the load (hitch inverts)

Tautline Hitch

For decades the Tautline hitch has been the standard "climbers' knot" used to self belay the climber ascending or descending on the climbing line. It is tied with a separate rope, of the same diameter as the climbing line, when using the split-tail system or the tail of the same rope when using the traditional climbing system. It is relatively fast to tie and can even be done with one hand. Extra wraps provide more friction and increase its holding potential.

The Tautline does have limitations which require certain precautions in order to avoid frustration and potential knot failure. The Taultline hitch tends to bind and tighten on the climbing line, sometimes requiring it to be loosened. Furthermore, after use the hitch tends to roll, lengthening the "bridge," sometimes to the point where the friction hitch is out of reach. With this in mind, tie the hitch with a slightly shorter bridge to allow for this situation. In addition, it is essential that a Figure Eight stopper knot be tied in the end of the remaining tail to prevent the knot from slipping apart. Even when taking these precautions, the Tautline will require frequent adjustment and attention. For these reasons many climbers are turning more frequently to the Blake's hitch.

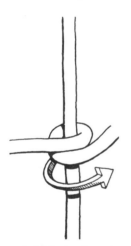 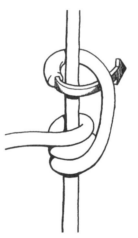 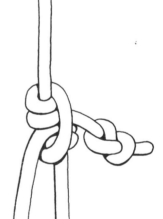

1 Make two turns below the bridge around the climbing line.

2 Continuing in the same direction, make two more turns above the bridge around the climbing line.

3 Dress and set the hitch as shown, so it grips the climbing line without slipping. A Figure Eight stopper knot is a must with this hitch.

Helpful Hint: Heat damage to the cord used to tie the friction hitch can be prevented during a descent on a dynamic climbing line system by first releasing and slightly loosening the hitch and using one of the following methods: 1) descend on a loosely formed foot lock on the climbing line; 2) descend on a Munter hitch tied to a pear-shaped locking carabiner attached to the saddle at a point below the friction hitch (a leg strap works well). Both methods are effective with any of the friction hitches used as a self belay.

Blake's Hitch

The Blake's hitch is a relative newcomer to the climbing scene, but it has been around long enough to prove itself worthy. The origin of this hitch is debatable, but it is firmly agreed that Jason Blake introduced and popularized it as an outstanding alternative to the Tautline hitch. Although identical in function to the Tautline, the Blake's hitch performs significantly better and has few limitations. Unlike the Tautline hitch, the Blake's hitch does not bind or tighten on the climbing line which allows for a smoother running friction hitch. This is especially noticeable when using a micro pulley as a slack tender device. In addition, the tail does not creep or roll, therefore preventing a lengthening bridge and a friction hitch that becomes out of reach. A Figure Eight stopper knot is still recommended in the tail of the rope.

The Blake's hitch is, however, slightly more difficult and slower to tie than the Tautline and cannot be tied with one hand. The most common mistake climbers make in tying this hitch is neglecting to pass the tail *between* the bridge and the climbing line (Fig. 2) before exiting through the first and second turns. In addition, the Blake's hitch has a high potential for causing friction damage to the section of tail that runs through the bottom turn of the hitch as it slides along the climbing line during descent. To reduce this effect, descend slowly.

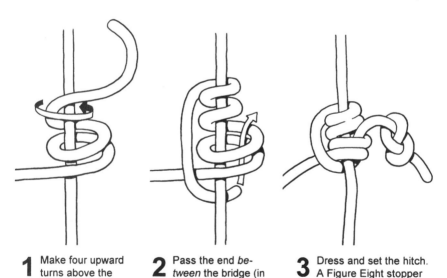

1 Make four upward turns above the bridge around the climbing line.

2 Pass the end *between* the bridge (in front) and the climbing line (behind) and up through the first two turns.

3 Dress and set the hitch. A Figure Eight stopper knot is recommended in the tail of the rope.

Helpful Hint: Make the first two turns of the hitch around your thumb. This creates a tunnel for the tail to be easily passed though.

French Prusik (Machard Tresse & Valdôtain Tresse)

For years, the French Prusik has been employed by mountaineers and rescue teams in France and Europe. Only recently has it received attention from tree climbers. Francois Dussenne from Belgium introduced this climbing hitch at a European Tree Climbing Competition in 1993. Since then the French Prusik has been showing up more frequently at tree climbing competitions and the work place alike. Most converts claim they won't go back to anything else.

The French Prusik is considered an advanced, high performance knot that will outperform any of the other friction hitches in most applications. Climbers that use the French Prusik immediately notice how quickly it grabs the rope when loaded and yet so easily releases afterward. The French Prusik is an elegant knot that is easy to tie and untie, inspect, and adjust. When used with a micro pulley, as a slack tender, the French Prusik advances without effort. Finally, because the hitch distributes the load over a longer distance of rope, it can safely support a greater working load than the other hitches.

However, the French Prusik is an unforgiving knot that has shortcomings with potentially fatal consequences. The primary shortcoming is that it some-times fails to grab the rope if not tied exactly right. This typically occurs when not enough wraps and braids are taken with the cord. The length, diameter, and pliability of the cord also strongly influence how the hitch will perform. As with all knots, the French Prusik must not be integrated into a climbing system until the climber has mastered tying and operating it while on the ground.

There are two variations of the French Prusik: the Machard tresse (M.t.) and the Valdôtain tresse (V.t.). The M.t. is tied to the rope with a Prusik loop or webbing sling and the V.t. is tied with a single length of cord or webbing with end-line attachment knots or eye splices. The knot is tied the same for both.

The Versatile Friction Hitch

Knots are tree climbers most versatile tool. The variety of friction hitches used as "rope grabs" are perhaps the most versatile knots of all. Friction hitches are the work horse of a climbing system, functioning as an ascender, belay device, and descender. Friction hitches also make excellent mid-line attachment points for a variety of climbing and rigging applications. In fact, they perform the job better than the mid-line knots because of their ability to slide along the rope, allowing for quick and easy adjustment. Even tubular webbing can be used as a rope grab when tied to the rope with either the Klemheist knot or French Prusik. And, when tied to a personal lanyard, friction hitches make great length adjusters.

The friction hitch is often employed in situations that are abusive to the rope used to tie the knot. Therefore, it is critical that the material used to tie them be in-spected often. When glazed and worn spots are found along the material, caused from heat and abrasion, it is time for replacement.

Tying the Valdôtain Tresse

Currently, the V.t. is the more popular of the two French Prusik variations with professional tree climbers. The diameter of the cord used for tying the V.t. to a 1/2 inch rope should be between 5/16 inch (8 mm) and 3/8 inch (9mm). Cord length will vary between 48-54 inch (untied), depending on its diameter and how many wraps and braids are used. If the cord is too short there will be too much friction and it will not slide smoothly—too long and the cord will slip. The difference is subtle, so experiment with and adjust the length accordingly.

Both the M.t. and V.t. consist of a series wraps (above) and braids (below). There are two ways to configure the braids: with the same leg of the cord always crossing on top of the other (as described below) or by alternating the crossings. Climbers are split over which one performs best, but both are acceptable, and for most, little, if any difference is noticed. Before tying the V.t., make attachment loops in the cord using the Double Fisherman's Loop.

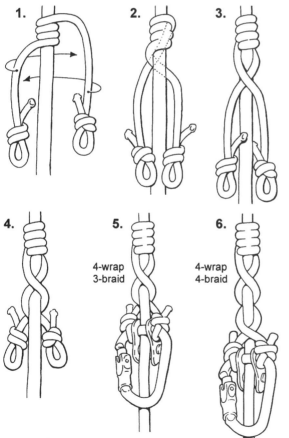

1. 2. 3.

4. 5. 6.

4-wrap 3-braid

4-wrap 4-braid

1 Begin by taking four wraps around the climbing line. Adjust the wraps so each leg of the cord is about the same length when hanging down.

2 Form the first braid by crossing the top cord over the bottom cord.

3 Form the second braid on the front side of the knot, by crossing the top cord over the bottom cord.

4 The third braid is formed by repeating step 3. The crossing will be on the back of the knot.

5 Clip the carabiner through each eye of the cord and micro pulley. Dress and set the knot by alternately pulling down and up on the carabiner.

6 If more friction is desired, additional braids can be taken by alternately crossing one leg of the cord over the other. Dress and set as above.

85

Prusik Knot

Another "must know" knot for the tree climber is the Prusik knot. If you have already learned the Girth hitch, this one will be easy. The Prusik is nothing more than a series of Girth hitches—one wrapped inside the other. The Prusik knot is used to attach a Prusik loop to a single or doubled climbing line. This loop functions as a self belay when the climber enters the tree using the SRT, secured footlock method, or descends on a Figure eight device. Never use the Prusik knot, or any other friction hitch, as the sole means for descending when using a static climbing line system. The only exception is when using a dynamic climbing system.

Applications for the Prusik loop/knot are almost limitless. It can be used as a split tail, lanyard adjuster, mid-rope anchor point for rigging, or an alternative rope grab device anywhere an ascender might be employed. The Prusik knot can also be tied to the climbing line with a tail of rope when using the traditional or split-tail climbing system. (A Figure Eight stopper knot in the tail is recommended.)

The gripping potential of the Prusik is increased by creating more friction. Adding more wraps to the knot will accomplish that. The number will vary depending on the stiffness and diameter of the cord being used to tie the knot and the rope it is being tied to. Inspect and replace worn Prusik loops and split tails frequently.

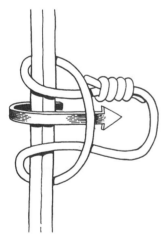

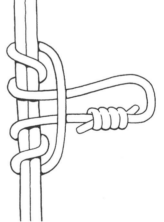

1 Begin by making a single Girth hitch around the doubled (or single) climbing line with the Prusik loop. Position the Double Fisherman's knot so it won't interfere with knot tying and carabiner attachment.

2 Make two more complete turns with the Prusik loop through the center of the original Girth hitch. Three wraps (six coils) is usually considered minimum in most instances.

3 Dress and set the hitch. Ensure that the hitch "grabs" the line properly by loading it slowly.

Klemheist

The Klemheist (pronounced Clem-heist) is used in most of the same applications and tied with the same loop of rope as the Prusik knot. Oddly enough this friction hitch is used less frequently by tree climbers than the Prusik, even though it is faster and easier to tie and untie. The climbers who have used it have discovered that it slides more smoothly, loosens easier, and is less likely to jam than the Prusik knot. The amount of friction can be controlled by increasing or decreasing the number of turns. Like the Prusik, three turns should be considered minimum in most instances. The Klemheist is also an excellent hitch when using a webbing sling as a rope grab. When tied with webbing it will require more turns to grip the rope than is required with Prusik cord.

Unlike the Prusik, the Klemheist is not symmetrical in design and therefore it becomes a different knot—the Kreuzklem (Croys-clem) when the direction of the load is reversed. The Kreuzklem is still an effective friction hitch but the configuration is different which could slightly affect its performance.

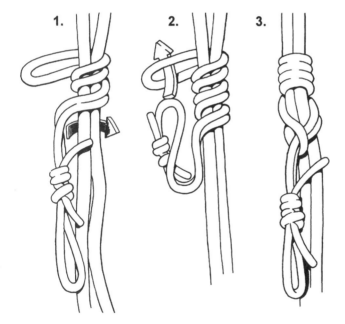

1 Make three downward turns around the climbing line. Position the Double Fisherman's knot so it won't conflict with knot tying and carabiner attachment.

2 Pass the lower end of the Prusik loop up through the top loop.

3 Align all the rope parts correctly and set the knot. Test the hitch to ensure that it properly grabs the rope.

"Breaking" a Prusik and Klemheist Knot

After the Prusik or Klemheist has been loaded and tightened while climbing, the climber may wish to "break" or loosen the knot, so it can slide freely along the climbing line. To perform this task, take a footlock on the climbing line to unload the hitch and thumb the bridge of the knot away from the wraps and towards the other end of the Prusik loop. Slide the hitch to the new position and reset.

Butterfly Knot

It is often desirable to have an attachment point in the rope, other than in the ends. This requires the use of a mid-line knot tied on the bight, and for many climbers and riggers the Butterfly knot is their first choice. Also referred to as the Single Lineman's Loop, the Butterfly can be tied and untied quickly and easily. And, because of its symmetry, can be easily inspected and loaded from either direction. It is important to set and dress this knot properly as it tends to jam under heavier loads.

The Butterfly knot is used during cabling and tree removal operations for attaching come-alongs, carabiners and pulleys, or when used by itself, as the loop for a Trucker's hitch. The latter application allows the user to set up mechanical advantage (MA) systems by passing the rope through the knot itself. The MA can be increased by adding more knots in the appropriate location. Compared to using carabiners and pulleys in a MA system, the effectiveness of this method is slightly diminished because of the increased rope friction.

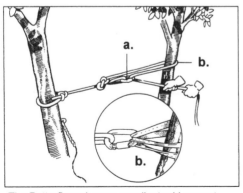

The Butterfly makes an excellent mid-rope attachment point for creating a 3-to-1 MA system. By using carabiners at the attachment point (a) and the anchor point (b), friction will be reduced and improve the effectiveness of the system.

1 Make a 360-degree twist in a bight of rope, forming an eye. Bring the end of the bight downwards...

2 ...and pass between the legs of the standing part and up through the eye.

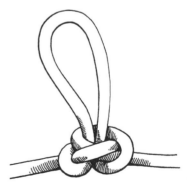

3 Pull on the end of the bight and both standing parts to tighten.

Bowline on a Bight

Another excellent mid-line knot is the Bowline on a Bight (BOAB)—a variation of the Bowline. It is perhaps, one of the first climbing harnesses professional tree climbers used. It still makes a satisfactory emergency harness for work or rescue by inserting a leg in each loop.

More commonly, the BOAB is applied the same way as the Butterfly knot. Although a bit tricky to learn at first, the BOAB is a pleasure to untie after excessive loading has occurred and is, for this reason and in this application, a better choice than the Butterfly knot. The loops formed from the BOAB can be used as a single attachment point or as two separate attachment points when setting up, for example, a 5-to-1 mechanical advantage system.

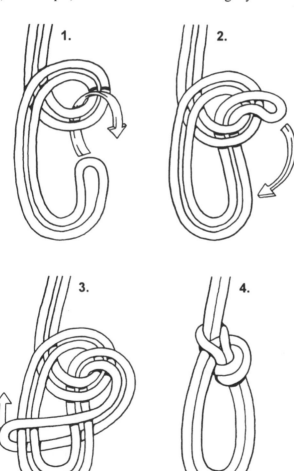

1 Form a loop with a bight of rope. Pass the end of the bight up though the loop.

2 Pass the bight downwards while opening the end.

3 Encircle the entire knot with the opened end of the bight until it reaches the standing part.

4 Pull on both standing parts and the sides that lead to the end of the bight. Dress and set this knot carefully.

The Bowline on a Bight can be easily untied by first loosening it and then rolling the bight back from the double standing part, downward around the double loops.

Double Fisherman's Knot (Grapevine Knot)

For the tree climber, the primary application of the Double Fisherman's knot is to make Prusik loops. Keep in mind, when making them, to factor in the extra cord length for tying the knots. A three foot Prusik loop tied in 3/8 inch diameter cord will require a total of eight feet of cord—two feet for the knots and six for the loop. The ends of the knot may be finished by taping, tying (Constrictor knot), whipping, or stitching to prevent accidental snagging.

1 Pass one end of the rope around the standing part of the other end twice, forming a figure 8, and insert the end through the loops (1a). Repeat the above procedure with the other end (1b), but in the opposite direction, so the finished knots are parallel to each other.

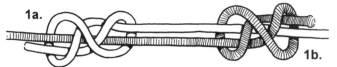

2 Tighten each knot separately by pulling on the end and the standing part. Join the two knots by pulling both standing parts located outside the knots.

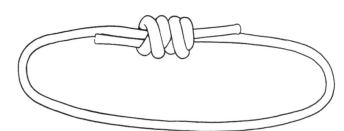

3 The finished knot should have one end above the standing part and one below the standing part. The remaining tails should be about three inches long.

The Fisherman's Backup

For added safety and neatness, the tree climber can backup attachment knots such as the Figure Eight on a Bight or Buntline hitch with the Fisherman's knot, or more specifically, half of the Double Fisherman's knot.

It should be tied close to the main knot and around the standing part of the line. If the tail is too short for tying the Fisherman's knot, tie an Overhand knot instead. Avoid using half hitches for a backup as they come untied easily.

Sliding Double Fisherman's Knot

Tracing the origins of knots is sometimes a difficult thing to do—as in the case of the Sliding Double Fisherman's knot (SDFK). It is starting to appear in climbing circles around the world, with no hint of its inventor. Nevertheless, this knot is an outstanding alternative to the Double Fisherman's knot (DFK) for the climber who desires a Prusik loop with an adjustable eye in the end. This feature allows the eye to be snugged tightly against a carabiner, preventing it from moving. Also, the SDFK does not get in the way when tying the Prusik loop to the rope or conflict with carabiner attachment, like the DFK sometimes does. So far only a few strength tests have been performed on this knot. They indicate only a slightly lower breaking strength with this knot than with the DFK. When making Prusik loops, allow a few extra inches beyond that which is required for tying the DFK.

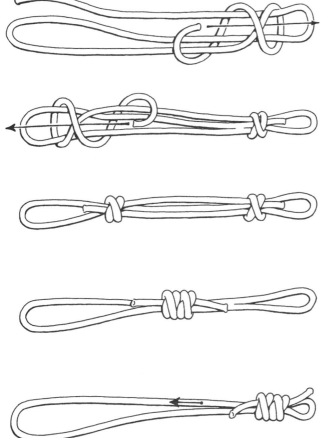

1 Lay the cord out in the shape of the letter Z. Tie one half of a Double Fisherman's knot around all three "legs" or strands of the cord.

2 Repeat the above procedure with the other end but in the opposite direction.

3 Set each knot separately by pulling on the end and the standing part.

4 Join the knots by first locating the standing parts that will draw the knots together. Pull on those standing parts, taking out slack, until the two knots are snug against each other.

5 Form an eye in one end of the loop by pulling on the standing part that slides.

Water Knot (Ring Bend)

The most commonly used knot for joining the ends of webbing together to form slings (endless loops) is the Water knot. It is simple to tie and easy to inspect. It is important to properly dress, set, and load the knot before use to prevent the ends from creeping and the knot from coming untied. Leave a three inch tail on each side of the knot. After heavy loading this knot becomes difficult to untie. It can sometimes be loosened by rolling the knot between the palms of the hand and untied by gripping together the standing part and end of each side and pushing towards each other.

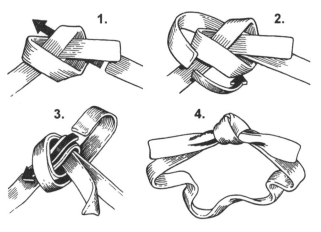

1 Tie an Overhand knot in one end of the webbing.

2 Match the other end of the webbing to the first end.

3 Retrace the original Overhand knot.

4 Dress and set. Tails should exit from opposite sides of the knot and be about 3 inches long.

The Daisy Chain

One of the best ways to store webbing slings and Prusik loops (and rope when washing) is with the Daisy Chain technique. The chained sling is easily unraveled by unlocking the final tuck of material and giving a quick yank on the end.

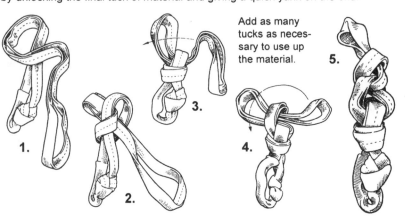

Add as many tucks as necessary to use up the material.

Beer Knot

If you want a webbing sling that is significantly stronger, neater, and more compact than the Water knot, use the Beer knot. This knot is actually a combination of a bend and a splice. It retains 80% of the original strength of the webbing. This knot was first introduced at a National Speleological Society Convention in the late 1980's by Peter Ludwig of Austria. Although relatively new, the knot's strength has been extensively tested. The Beer knot does, however, require more time and effort to tie than the water knot.

There are a few tricks that make tying the Beer knot a bit easier. First, heat seal the receiving end of the webbing "open" to create a tunnel for the other end. The end to be inserted should not be heat sealed, but rather cut with scissors or a knife. (Heat sealing creates a sharp edge that can catch on the inside of the webbing.) Secondly, fold the end to be inserted in half, lengthwise, to make it stiffer and easier to insert. It may be necessary to use a small chain saw file, for example, as a poker to insert the one end into the other.

1 Tie an Overhand knot in a length of webbing.

2 Insert 10 to 12 inches of one end of the webbing into the hollow of the other end.

3 Work the Overhand knot around the sling to the overlap area. Set and dress.

Note: The discussion on making webbing slings is covered in more detail on page 62.

The Strength of Webbing

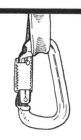

"Webbing is susceptible to the same normal vector forces as ropes. In this application, when webbing is wrapped around a small diameter anchor or forms a small angle with the connecting carabiner, its strength approaches the strength of the two legs combined. Numerous tests by a number of reputable disbelieving groups have discovered that 20 kN (4,000 lbf.) webbing when doubled over a carabiner of fair diameter, will yield almost 40 kN (8,000 lbf) of strength".

From *On Rope* by Bruce Smith and Allen Padgett

Sources of Information

The most accomplished tree climbers are often the ones who seek instruction, acquire knowledge, and stay informed. The sources of information listed below will enable the inspired climber to accomplish all of those pursuits.

Organizations

International Society of Arboriculture (ISA)
P.O. Box 3129, Champaign, IL 61826
888-472-8733
www.isa-arbor.com

Tree Care Industry Association
136 Harvey Rd., Suite 101, Londonderry NH 03053, 800-733-2622
www.treecareindustry.com

Tree Climber's International (TCI)
P.O. Box 5588
Atlanta, GA 31107
404-377-3150
www.treeclimbing.com
Contact: Peter Jenkins

Training

ArborMaster
P.O. Box 62, Willington, CT 06279
860-429-5028, www.arbormaster.com

Arboriculture Canada Training & Education LTD
1 McLeod Crescent, Olds, Alberta, T4H 1E9, Canada
877-268-8733, www.arborcanada.com

North American Training Solutions
910 Athens Hwy. Suite K219
Loganville, GA 30052, 888-652-9116
www.northamericantraining solutions.com

Proclimber
United Kingdom, Tel: 1558 685862
www.proclimber.co.uk

Tree Climber's International (TCI)
(see listing under "Organizations")

Books

American National Standards Institute, *ANSI Z133-2012. American National Standard for Arboriculture Operations—Safety Requirements.* International Society of Arboriculture.

American National Standards Institute, *ANSI A300 (Part 1)-2008 Pruning. Tree, Shrub, and Other Woody Plant Maintenance—Standard Practices (Pruning).* New York, NY

Ashley, Clifford W, *The Ashley Book of Knots.* New York: Doubleday, and London, 1944.

Beranek, Gerald, *The Fundamentals of General Tree Work.* Fort Bragg, CA: Beranek Publications, 1996.
www.atreestory.com

Bigon, Mario & Guido Regazzoni, *The Morrow Guide to Knots.* New York: Morrow and Co., 1981.

Blair, Don, *Arborist Equipment: A Guide to the Tools and Equipment for Tree Maintenance and Removal (Second Edition).* Champaign, IL: International Society of Arboriculture, 1995.

Budworth, Geoffrey, *The Complete Book of Knots.* New York, NY: Lyons and Burford, 1999.

Frank, James and Jerrold Smith, *CMC Rope Rescue Manual.* Santa Barbara, CA: CMC Rescue Inc., 1998.

International Society of Arboriculture, *Quick Reference Guide of Arboriculture Terms: English-Spanish/ Spanish-English.* Champaign, IL: International Society of Arboriculture, 1999.

Jepson, Jeff, *Knots at Work.* Longville, MN: Beaver Tree Publishing, 2013.

Jepson, Jeff, *To Fell a Tree.* Longville, MN: Beaver Tree Publishing, 2009.

Lilly, Sharon, *Tree Climber's Guide.* Champaign, IL: International Society of Arboriculture, 2005 (3rd edition). Also available in Spanish.

Luebben, Craig, *Knots for Climbers.* Evergreen, CO: Chockstone Press, Inc., 1995.

Matheny, Nelda and James R. Clark, *A Photographic Guide to the Evaluation of Hazard Trees in Urban Areas, 2nd Edition.* Champaign, IL: Int. Society of Arboriculture, 1994.

Tree Care Industry Association, *A Climber's Guide to Hazard Trees.* Amherst, NH: Tree Care Industry Association, 1993.

Raleigh, Duane, *Knots and Ropes for Climbers.* Mechanicsburg, PA: Stackpole Books, 1998.

Smith, Bruce and Allen Padgett, *On Rope.* Huntsville, AL: National Speleological Society, 1996.

Toss, Brion, *Chapman's Nautical Guides: Knots.* New York: Hearst Marine Books, 1990.

Toss, Brion, *The Complete Rigger's Apprentice.* Camden, ME: International Marine/McGraw-Hill, 1998.

Vines, Tom and Steve Hudson. *High Angle Rescue Techniques, 2nd Edition.* St. Louis, MO: Mosby, Inc., 1999.

Magazines

Arb Climber, Aerial Arboriculture, PPE, Climbing and Cutting Equipment www.arbclimber.com

Arbor Age: Published monthly by Green Media, www.arborage.com.

Arborist News: Published six times a year by the International Society of Arboriculture.

The Tree Worker: Published monthly by the Tree Care Industry Association.

Tree Care Industry: The official publication of the Tree Care Industry Association.

Videos

Tree Climbing Basics (DVD): Hosted by Peter "Treeman" Jenkins, the father of recreational tree climbing. Available through Tree Climbers International (see listing on page 94).

ArborMaster Training Video Series I, II, and III: A series of 14 training videos for the professional tree climber about climbing techniques, equipment, maintenance, and knots. ISA, 1997-1998. Includes workbooks.

Basic Training for Tree Climbers: A five-video set that teaches the fundamentals of production tree climbing. Jointly produced by the ISA and TCIA, 1999. Includes workbook.

Rigging for Removal: A two-video set about rigging techniques and equipment. Produced by the TCIA, 1998. Includes workbook.

Working Climber DVD Series: Three different series are available covering access and movement in the tree and cutting and rigging in the tree. Beranek Publications. www.atreestory.com

Arborist Equipment Suppliers

The listing below includes some of the suppliers of the equipment and supplies used by the professional tree climber and worker. Many of these suppliers will provide descriptive and informative product catalogs upon request.

Alexander Equipment Company
4728 Yender Ave., Lisle, IL 60532
630-663-1400, www.alexequip.com

American Arborist Supplies, Inc.
882 South Matlack Street, West Chester, PA 19382, 800-441-8381
www.arborist.com

American Chainsaws & 2 Cycle Inc.
3531 Lawrenceville Hwy.,
Tucker, GA 30084, 770-934-7297
www.americanchainsawtuckerga.com

A.M. Leonard, Inc.
P.O. Box 816, 241 Fox Drive,
Piqua, OH 45356, 800-543-8955
www.amleo.com

Arbor Tech Supply
11494 James Madison Street
Remington, VA 22734, 877-506-8733
www.arbortechsupply.com

Arborwear®
8269 E. Washington St., Chagrin Falls,
OH 40023, 888-578-8733
www.arborwear.com

Artistic Arborist, Inc.
4519 N. 7th Ave., Phoenix, AZ 85013
800-782-8733 or 602-263-8889
www.artistic-arborist.com

Bailey's (Home Office)
1222 Palmers Ave, Suite D, Woodland,
CA 95766, 800-322-4539
www.baileys-online.com

Bartlett Manufacturing Company
7876 S. Van Dyke, Marlette, MI
48453, 800-331-7101
www.bartlettman.com

Bishop Company
P.O. Box 870, 12519 E. Putnam Street,
Whittier, CA 90602, 800-421-4833
www.bishco.com

K&M Lawn, Garden, & Arb. Supplies
16033 Ira Hoffman Lane,
Culpeper, VA 22701, 800-577-8733
www.blueridgearboristsupply.com

Buckingham Manufacturing Co. Inc.
1-11 Travis Avenue, P.O. Box 1690
Binghamton, NY 13902, 607-773-2400
www.buckinghammfg.com

Cleaves Co.
300 Reservior St., Needham, MA
02494, 877-449-0833
www.cleavesco.com

Forestry Suppliers, Inc.
205 West Rankin St., P.O. Box 8397,
Jackson, MS 39284-8397, 800-647-
5368, www.forestry-suppliers.com

Kramer Equipment Company, Inc.
7835 Richmond Hwy., Alexandria, VA
22306, 800-500-7835
www.kramerequip.com

Lanphear Supply
1884 S. Green Road, Cleveland, OH
44121, 800-332-8733 or 216-381-1704
www.lanphearsupply.com

Metro Arborist Supplies
6565 Coffman Road, Indianapolis, IN
46268, 877-408-7337
www.treestuff.com

Midwest Arborist Supplies
P.O. Box 151455, Grand Rapids, MI
49515, 800-423-3789
www.treecaresupplies.com

Newtown Power Equipment
151 Mount Pleasant Rd., Newtown, CT
06470, 203-426-5012
www.newtownpowerequipment.com

New Tribe, Inc (recreational climbing)
P.O. Box 638, Grants Pass, OR 97528,
866-223-3371, www.newtribe.com

Northeastern Arborist Supply
50 Notch Rd., Woodland Park, NJ
07424, 800-261-7772
www.northeasternarborist.com

On Rope 1, Inc.
5940-C, Hwy. 58, Harrison, TN 37341,
423-344-4716, www.onrope1.com

Rescue Response Gear
14916 Surrey Lane, Sisters, OR 97759
888-600-9116
www.rescueresponsegear.com

Shelter Tree Inc./Tree Care Products
195 John Dietsch Square, North Attle-
boro, MA 02763, 800-720-8733
www.sheltertree.com

Sherrill, Inc.
200 E. Seneca Road, Greensboro, NC
27406, 800-525-8873
www.sherrilltree.com

Sierra Moreno Mercantile Co.
19414-D, Leitersburg, MD 21742
800-262-0800, www.sierramoreno.com

WesSpur Tree Equipment, Inc.
2121 Iron St., Bellingham, WA 98225,
800-268-2141, www.wesspur.com

Westech Rigging Supply
Eugene, OR, 800-442-7454
www.westechrigging.com

Western Tree Equipment
11353 Sunrise Gold Circle, Suite I,
Rancho Cordova, CA 95742
800-942-7267, www.westerntree.biz

International Suppliers

Arborist Supply Company, Inc.
Bay 8, 141 Commercial Dr., Calgary,
Alberta, Canada T3Z 2A7, Tel: 888-
240-3993 (in Canada), 888-240-3993
(outside)
www.arboristsupplyco.ca

**Australian Tree & Rope Access
Equipment Specialists**
Australia, www.atraes.com.au

Buxtons Ltd.
United Kingdom, Tel: 01785 712397
www.buxtons.net

Fletcher Stewart Limited
United Kingdom, Tel: 0161 483 5542
www.fletcherstewart.com

Landmark Trading
United Kingdom, Tel: 01780 482231
www.landmarktrading.com

New Age Arbor Products
Victoria, Australia, Tel: 13000 27267
www.newagearbor.com.au

Pacific Arborist Supplies
#154 Riverside Drive W., North Van-
couver, British Columbia, Canada V7H
1T9, Tel: 604-929-6133 (in Canada)
888-996-2299 (outside)
www.pacificarborist.com

Safety Green
Boulder 1d, NL-6582 BZ Heumen,
Netherlands, Tel: +31 (0) 24-3977583

Tree Gear Arborist Supplies
Victoria, Australia, Tel: 1300 319 918
www.treegear.com.au

Treesource
United Kingdom, Tel: 01904 720126
www.treesource.co.uk

Skill Performance Sheet

Skill performance sheets are a convenient method of recording the climbing skills and techniques the climber has learned. The climber's demonstration of competence of the listed performance items can be recorded however the employer, employee, instructor, or student desires (dates, checkmarks, etc.). By making duplicate copies of the performance sheets the employer and the climber can simultaneously keep track of his or her progress. Use the page numbers as an index to quickly locate the performance item listed.

Student _____ **Evaluator** _____

Pre-Climb Inspection

Performance Guidelines	Performed
1. Name/describe the function of the climbing gear on page 9.	
2. Recite the P.R.E.P. system. Name the components. (p. 10)	
3. Inspect personal protective equipment (visual/verbal). (p. 12)	
4. Inspect climbing/rigging lines and split tails (visual/verbal). (p. 12)	
5. Inspect climbing saddle (visual/verbal). (p. 13)	
6. Inspect lanyards and Prusik loops (visual/verbal). (p. 13)	
7. Inspect connecting devices (visual/verbal). (p. 13)	
8. Inspect ascenders, descenders, false crotchs, redirects, and pulleys (visual/verbal). (p. 13)	
9. Locate the tree and site hazards in the illustration. (p. 16)	
10. Perform a visual tree inspection of root zone, trunk, and tree crown. Verbalize actions and findings. (pp. 16-17)	
11. Perform a visual inspection of the climbing and work site. Verbalize actions and findings. (pp. 16-17)	
12. Verbalize the job description, location of work to be performed, and the order for executing the work. (p. 18)	
13. Have all necessary climbing/rescue gear at the site. (p. 18)	
14. Locate drop zone. Take precautions to make work site safe. (p. 18)	
15. Select a suitable entry route and an entry method that is appropriate for the tree and work situation. (p. 18)	

Student _____ Evaluator _____

Rope Installation

Performance Guidelines	Performed
1. Recite an acceptable command and reply response system. (p. 58)	
2. Select a throwline & throwbag suitable for the limb/crotch. (p. 20)	
3. Demonstrate attaching the throwline to the throwbag. (p. 22)	
4. Demonstrate proper throwing procedure (wear personal protective equipment, prepare line, secure site, and alert others). (p. 21)	
5. Install throwline (ft) using the single hand toss. (p. 21)	
6. Install throwline (ft) using the cradle throw. (p. 21)	
7. Install throwline (ft) using the Big Shot. (p. 23)	
8. Demonstrate attaching throwline to the climbing line. (p. 22)	
9. Properly perform the strumming technique. (p. 24)	
10. Isolate throwline around a single limb using the single or double throwbag technique. (p. 24)	
11. Isolate throwline around a single limb using the stick trick. (p. 25)	
12. Position the climbing line by hand "flipping." (p. 26)	
13. Position the climbing line using the "flip stick." (p. 26)	
14. Install a line (ft) using a throwing knot: open form. (p. 31)	
15. Install a line (ft) using a throwing knot: closed form. (p. 31)	
16. Install a line (ft) using the Noose knot. (p. 32)	
17. Install climbing line (ft) using a pole saw or pruner. (p. 33)	
18. Properly install false crotch using method #1. (p. 28)	
19. Properly install false crotch using method #2. (p. 29)	
20. Properly retrieve false crotch using a throwline. (p. 28)	
21. Properly install rope saver. (p. 30)	
22. Properly retrieve rope saver using a throwline. (p. 30)	
23.	
24.	

Student _____ Evaluator _____

Entering the Tree

Performance Guidelines	Performed
1. Verbalize the application of each of the six entry methods.	
2. Properly set up ladder against a tree. (p. 36)	
3. Enter tree using a ladder: with installed line and ground belay.*	
4. Enter tree using a ladder: with installed line using a self belay.*	
5. Enter tree using a ladder: no belay, demonstrate safe technique.*	
6. Enter tree using the alternate lanyard technique. Must always be tied in during the climb and maintain three-point contact.* (p.37)	
7. Demonstrate proper setup and use of a hip Prusik lanyard. (p. 38)	
8. Demonstrate proper setup and use of a camming lanyard. (p. 38)	
9. Demonstrate Becket bend method of lanyard adjustment. (p. 39)	
10. Enter tree using the body thrust technique.* (p. 40)	
11. Perform the modified body thrust technique (using feet).* (p. 41)	
12. Perform the modified body thrust technique (using foot loop).*	
13. Enter tree using the secured footlock technique. Properly tie Prusik loop. Observe and verbalize Prusik loop limitations.* (p. 43)	
14. Setup single rope technique: 1) anchor climbing line to tree base 2) anchor line to limb (both with Running Bowline). (pp. 44, 76)	
15. Verbalize climbing line anchoring precautions. (p. 45)	
16. Properly attach ascender(s), with backup, to climbing line. (p. 47)	
17. Verbalize/perform ascender precautions. (p. 47)	
18. Enter tree using the "sit-stand" SRT.* (p. 46)	
19. Enter tree using climbing spurs. Demonstrate proper climbing, limb passing, and backup technique.* (pp. 48-49)	
20. Properly set up an adjustable false crotch (AFC). (p. 50)	
21. Use the AFC with a suitable entering/climbing technique. (p. 50)	
22.	

* Climber has a minimum of two means of tying in to the tree available.

Student _____ Evaluator _____

Positioning in the Tree

Performance Guidelines	Performed
1. Select a safe and effective tie-in point in the canopy. (p.52)	
2. Select a suitable natural crotch and install a climbing line. (p. 52)	
3. Install a climbing line using a false crotch device. (pp. 28,52)	
4. Properly tie in using the traditional climbing system. (p. 53-54)	
5. Properly tie in using the split-tail climbing system. (pp. 53-54)	
6. Attach and operate a slack tender with climbing system. (p. 55)	
7. Advance climbing line using alternate lanyard technique. (p.37)	
8. Advance climbing line using a throwline. (pp. 20,56)	
9. Advance climbing line using a throwing knot. (pp. 31-32)	
10. Advance climbing line using a pole saw or pruner. (p. 33)	
11. Demonstrate good limb walking technique (going out/in). (p. 57)	
12. Recrotch climbing line to a new location in the tree. (p. 58)	
13. Install/work from a double crotch in a suitable situation. (p. 59)	
14. Install/work from mechanical redirect in suitable situation. (p. 60)	
15. Install a "retrievable" redirect. Retrieve from ground. (p. 60)	
16. Install/work from a natural redirect in a suitable situation. (p. 61)	
17. Retrieve/reposition climbing line using a natural redirect. (p. 61)	
18. Perform a descent on a dynamic climbing line system. (p.64)	
19. Attach figure-8 device to rope and secure with a *soft lock*. (p. 66)	
20. Attach figure-8 device to rope and secure with a *hard lock*. (p. 66)	
21. Descend with figure-8: double static line with backup. (pp. 64-65)	
22. Descend with figure-8: single static line with backup. (pp. 64-65)	
23. Descend with Petzel *Stop* (or equal): single static line. (pp. 64-65)	
24. Clear rope from tree, alert others, and coil/stuff rope. (pp. 64,69)	
25.	

Note: Climber must be tied in with at least one means of attachment at all times.

Student _____ Evaluator _____

Attachment Knots

Performance Guidelines	Performed
1. Verbalize meaning/importance of tie, dress, set (TDS). (p. 67)	
2. Demonstrate and verbalize rope parts and terminology. (p. 69)	
3. Bowline (single): TDS. Use as tie in with TCS.* (p. 70)	
4. Bowline (Yosemite tie-off): TDS. Tie in with STCS.* (p. 70)	
5. Figure 8 (simple): TDS. Tie to throwbag. (p. 71)	
6. Figure 8 on a Bight: TDS. Use as tie in with TCS & STCS. (p. 71)	
7. Buntline Hitch: TDS. Use as tie in with TCS and STCS. (p. 72)	
8. Anchor Hitch: TDS. Use as tie in with TCS and STCS. (p. 73)	
9. Double-Fisherman's Loop: TDS. Use as tie in with STCS. (p. 74)	
10. Clove Hitch: TDS. Tie around a limb with 2 half hitches. (p. 75)	
11. Clove Hitch on a Bight: TDS. Tie in with TCS. (p. 75)	
12. Running Bowline: TDS. Tie around a limb for lowering. (p. 76)	
13. Cow Hitch: TDS. Use to attach an anchor sling to a tree. (p. 77)	
14. Girth Hitch: TDS. Use to attach a redirect sling to limb. (p. 77)	
15. Basket Hitch: TDS. Use to attach a redirect sling to limb. (p. 77)	
16. Timber Hitch: TDS. Use to attach an anchor sling to a tree. (p. 78)	
17. Sheet Bend: TDS with 2 ropes of different diameter. (p. 79)	
18. Slippery Sheet Bend: TDS with 2 ropes. Demonstrate quick release feature. (p. 79)	
19. Quick Hitch: TDS with 2 ropes. Demonstrate quick release feature. (p. 80)	
20. Pile Hitch: TDS. Use to attach thowline to rope. (p. 22)	
21.	
22.	
23.	

*TDS: Tie. dress. and set; TCS: Traditional climbing system; STCS: Split-tail climbing system

Student _____ Evaluator _____

Friction Hitches (Climbing Knots)

Performance Guidelines	Performed
1. Munter Hitch: TDS* on pear-shaped locking carabiner. (p. 81)	
2. Munter Hitch: Perform belay 1) climber 2) lowering limb. (p. 81)	
3. Tautline Hitch: TDS with Figure 8 stopper knot in tail. (p. 82)	
4. Blake's Hitch: TDS with Figure 8 stopper knot in tail. (p. 83)	
5. Machard tresse: TDS using a Prusik loop. (p. 85)	
6. Machard tresse: TDS using a webbing sling. (p. 85)	
7. Valdôtain tresse: TDS using Prusik cord. (p. 85)	
8. Prusik Knot: TDS using Prusik loop with three wraps. (p. 86)	
9. Prusik Knot: TDS using climbing line with TCS* and STCS.*	
10. Klemheist: TDS using Prusik loop with three wraps. (p. 87)	
11. Klemheist: TDS using webbing sling. (p. 87)	
12. "Break" Prusik and Klemheist knot as described in sidebar. (p. 87)	

Mid-Line Knots

1. Butterfly Knot: TDS. (p. 88)	
2. Bowline on a Bight: TDS. (p. 89)	
3. Setup 3-to-1 mechanical advantage using knots of choice. (p. 88)	

Bends (End-to-End Tie-Offs)

1. Double Fisherman's Knot: TDS using Prusik cord. (p. 90)	
2. Backup an attachment knot using the Fisherman's Backup. (p. 90)	
3. Sliding Double Fisherman's Knot: TDS using Prusik cord. (p. 91)	
4. Water Knot: TDS making a webbing sling. (p. 92)	
5. Beer Knot: TDS making a webbing sling. (p. 93)	
6. Demonstrate six different uses of a webbing sling. (pp. 62-63)	
7. Daisy Chain: Form chain using a webbing sling. (p. 92)	

*TDS: Tie. dress, and set; TCS: Traditional climbing system; STCS: Split-tail climbing system

DON'T MATTER WHO I WORK FOR
I'M STILL DRAG'N THE BRUSH.

About the Author

Jeff Jepson has a passion for trees and for climbing. A certified arborist and owner of Beaver Tree Service since 1989, he is a committed professional who values climbing education and professional development. He attends climbing workshops, competitions, and trade shows and believes that experienced climbers have much to offer one another and others who are interested in learning safe climbing techniques. You can often find him in trees even when he is not on the job. Twice Jeff has earned the title of All-Around Climbing Champion of the Minnesota Chapter of the ISA. Jeff lives near Longville, MN with his wife Bonnie and their two children, Luke and Anna. The Jepsons are very active in their church and community.

About the Illustrator

Bryan Kotwica is a commercial artist from Libertyville, Illinois whose illustrations appear regularly in Sherrill catalogs and in various National Arborist Association publications. He is also a professional climber who experiences daily the rigors of the climbing profession and the business end of the tree care industry. This unique combination makes Bryan the perfect illustrator for books such as The Tree Climber's Companion. Bryan's commitment to both professions is evident in the accuracy of his illustrations.

Visit us at: BeaverTreeMN.com